50 Soul Food Recipes for Home

By: Kelly Johnson

Table of Contents

- Fried Chicken
- Collard Greens
- Macaroni and Cheese
- Cornbread
- Black-eyed Peas
- Sweet Potato Pie
- Fried Catfish
- Biscuits and Gravy
- Hush Puppies
- Southern Fried Pork Chops
- Red Beans and Rice
- Shrimp and Grits
- BBQ Ribs
- Peach Cobbler
- Chicken and Waffles
- Candied Yams
- Banana Pudding
- Buttermilk Biscuits
- Okra Gumbo
- Crawfish Étouffée
- Jambalaya
- Southern Fried Green Tomatoes
- Cornbread Dressing
- Fried Okra
- Collard Greens with Ham Hocks
- Pulled Pork Sandwiches
- Fried Catfish Po' Boy
- Smothered Pork Chops
- Southern Style Green Beans
- Blackened Catfish
- Baked Macaroni and Cheese
- Cornbread Stuffing
- Fried Chicken Wings
- Sweet Potato Casserole
- Chicken Fried Steak

- Pecan Pie
- Chicken and Dumplings
- Grits with Cheese
- Southern Style Coleslaw
- Sweet Tea
- Buttermilk Fried Shrimp
- Country Fried Steak
- Bourbon Pecan Pie
- Dirty Rice
- Fried Oysters
- Texas Toast
- Collard Green and Black-eyed Pea Soup
- BBQ Pulled Pork
- Cajun Shrimp Pasta
- Baked Beans

Fried Chicken

Ingredients:

- 1 whole chicken, cut into pieces
- 2 cups buttermilk
- 2 cups all-purpose flour
- 1 tablespoon salt
- 1 tablespoon black pepper
- 1 teaspoon paprika
- 1 teaspoon garlic powder
- 1 teaspoon onion powder
- Vegetable oil, for frying

Instructions:

Marinate the Chicken:
- Place the chicken pieces in a large bowl and pour the buttermilk over them. Ensure all pieces are well coated. Cover and refrigerate for at least 4 hours, or overnight for best results.

Prepare the Coating:
- In a shallow dish or bowl, mix together the flour, salt, black pepper, paprika, garlic powder, and onion powder until well combined. This will be your seasoned flour mixture.

Coat the Chicken:
- Remove the marinated chicken from the refrigerator and let it sit at room temperature for about 30 minutes.
- Heat the vegetable oil in a large skillet or Dutch oven over medium-high heat until it reaches 350°F (175°C).
- While the oil is heating, dredge each piece of chicken in the seasoned flour mixture, shaking off any excess.

Fry the Chicken:
- Carefully place the coated chicken pieces in the hot oil, making sure not to overcrowd the pan. Fry in batches if necessary.
- Fry the chicken until golden brown and crispy, about 12-15 minutes for dark meat (thighs and drumsticks) and 10-12 minutes for white meat (breasts and wings).
- Use tongs to turn the chicken pieces occasionally to ensure even cooking.
- Once cooked through and crispy, transfer the fried chicken to a wire rack set over a baking sheet to drain excess oil.

Serve:
- Allow the fried chicken to rest for a few minutes before serving to allow the juices to redistribute.
- Serve hot, garnished with fresh herbs if desired, alongside your favorite sides like mashed potatoes, coleslaw, or biscuits.

Enjoy this classic Southern dish of crispy and juicy fried chicken with your loved ones!

Collard Greens

Ingredients:

- 2 bunches of collard greens
- 6 slices of bacon, chopped (or substitute with smoked turkey for a healthier option)
- 1 onion, finely chopped
- 3 cloves garlic, minced
- 4 cups chicken or vegetable broth
- 1 tablespoon apple cider vinegar
- 1 teaspoon sugar (optional)
- Salt and black pepper to taste
- Hot sauce (optional, for serving)

Instructions:

Prepare the Collard Greens:
- Wash the collard greens thoroughly under cold water. Remove the tough stems and ribs, then stack the leaves and chop them into bite-sized pieces. Set aside.

Cook the Bacon and Onion:
- In a large pot or Dutch oven, cook the chopped bacon over medium heat until it becomes crispy and renders its fat, about 5-7 minutes.
- Add the chopped onion to the pot and sauté until softened and translucent, about 3-4 minutes.
- Stir in the minced garlic and cook for an additional 1-2 minutes until fragrant.

Simmer the Greens:
- Add the chopped collard greens to the pot, stirring to coat them in the bacon fat and onion mixture.
- Pour in the chicken or vegetable broth until it just covers the greens. If needed, add water to ensure the greens are fully submerged.
- Stir in the apple cider vinegar and sugar (if using). Season with salt and black pepper to taste.

Cook Until Tender:
- Bring the pot to a boil, then reduce the heat to low. Cover and simmer the collard greens for 1 to 1.5 hours, stirring occasionally, until they are tender and flavorful.
- Taste and adjust seasoning as needed. If desired, add a dash of hot sauce for extra heat.

Serve:
- Once the collard greens are tender, they are ready to serve.
- Serve hot as a side dish alongside your favorite Southern meals, such as fried chicken, cornbread, or black-eyed peas.
- Enjoy the rich, smoky flavor of these classic Southern collard greens!

This recipe yields tender and flavorful collard greens that are perfect for any Southern-inspired meal. Adjust the seasonings and level of heat to suit your taste preferences.

Macaroni and Cheese

Ingredients:

- 8 oz (about 2 cups) elbow macaroni
- 4 tablespoons unsalted butter
- 1/4 cup all-purpose flour
- 2 cups whole milk
- 2 cups shredded sharp cheddar cheese
- 1 cup shredded mozzarella cheese
- 1/2 teaspoon salt
- 1/4 teaspoon black pepper
- 1/4 teaspoon paprika (optional)
- 1/4 cup breadcrumbs (optional, for topping)

Instructions:

Cook the Macaroni:
- Bring a large pot of salted water to a boil. Add the macaroni and cook according to the package instructions until al dente. Drain and set aside.

Make the Cheese Sauce:
- In a large saucepan, melt the butter over medium heat.
- Once melted, add the flour and whisk continuously until the mixture becomes smooth and bubbly, about 1-2 minutes.
- Gradually pour in the milk, whisking constantly to prevent lumps from forming.
- Cook the mixture, stirring frequently, until it thickens and begins to bubble, about 5-7 minutes.
- Reduce the heat to low and stir in the shredded cheddar and mozzarella cheese until melted and smooth. Season with salt, black pepper, and paprika, if using. Remove from heat.

Combine Macaroni and Cheese Sauce:
- Add the cooked macaroni to the cheese sauce, stirring until the pasta is evenly coated with the cheese mixture.

Bake (Optional):
- Preheat your oven to 350°F (175°C).
- Transfer the macaroni and cheese mixture to a greased baking dish.
- If desired, sprinkle breadcrumbs over the top for a crunchy topping.
- Bake in the preheated oven for 20-25 minutes, or until the top is golden brown and the cheese is bubbly.

Serve:
- Remove the macaroni and cheese from the oven and let it cool slightly before serving.

- Serve hot as a comforting main dish or as a side to your favorite meals.
- Enjoy the creamy and cheesy goodness of this classic macaroni and cheese recipe!

Feel free to customize this recipe by adding other types of cheese or additional ingredients like cooked bacon, diced ham, or chopped vegetables. Adjust the seasoning according to your taste preferences.

Cornbread

Ingredients:

- 1 cup yellow cornmeal
- 1 cup all-purpose flour
- 1/4 cup granulated sugar (optional, adjust to taste)
- 1 tablespoon baking powder
- 1/2 teaspoon baking soda
- 1/2 teaspoon salt
- 1 cup buttermilk
- 2 large eggs
- 1/2 cup unsalted butter, melted

Instructions:

Preheat the Oven:
- Preheat your oven to 400°F (200°C). Grease a 9-inch square baking dish or cast iron skillet with butter or cooking spray.

Mix Dry Ingredients:
- In a large mixing bowl, combine the cornmeal, flour, sugar (if using), baking powder, baking soda, and salt. Stir until well combined.

Combine Wet Ingredients:
- In a separate bowl, whisk together the buttermilk and eggs until smooth.

Combine Wet and Dry Ingredients:
- Pour the wet ingredients into the dry ingredients, along with the melted butter. Stir until just combined. Do not overmix; a few lumps are okay.

Bake:
- Pour the batter into the prepared baking dish or skillet, spreading it out evenly.
- Bake in the preheated oven for 20-25 minutes, or until the top is golden brown and a toothpick inserted into the center comes out clean.

Serve:
- Allow the cornbread to cool in the baking dish for a few minutes before slicing and serving.
- Serve warm with butter, honey, or your favorite toppings.
- Enjoy the classic, comforting taste of Southern cornbread!

This recipe yields a moist and slightly sweet cornbread with a tender crumb. Feel free to adjust the amount of sugar according to your preference for sweetness. You can also add additional ingredients like chopped jalapeños or grated cheese for extra flavor.

Black-eyed Peas

Ingredients:

- 2 cups dried black-eyed peas
- 6 cups water
- 1 onion, chopped
- 3 cloves garlic, minced
- 2 bay leaves
- 1 ham hock or smoked turkey leg (optional, for flavor)
- 1 teaspoon salt, or to taste
- 1/2 teaspoon black pepper
- 1/2 teaspoon smoked paprika (optional, for extra flavor)
- Hot sauce, for serving (optional)
- Chopped fresh parsley or green onions, for garnish (optional)

Instructions:

Prepare the Black-Eyed Peas:
- Rinse the dried black-eyed peas under cold water and pick out any debris or discolored peas.
- In a large pot or Dutch oven, combine the black-eyed peas and water. Let them soak for at least 4 hours or overnight.

Cook the Black-Eyed Peas:
- After soaking, drain and rinse the black-eyed peas again.
- Return the peas to the pot and add the chopped onion, minced garlic, bay leaves, and ham hock or smoked turkey leg, if using.
- Pour in enough water to cover the peas by about 1 inch.
- Bring the pot to a boil over medium-high heat, then reduce the heat to low and let the peas simmer, partially covered, for 45 minutes to 1 hour, or until tender. Stir occasionally and add more water if needed to keep the peas covered.

Season and Serve:
- Once the black-eyed peas are tender, remove the bay leaves and ham hock or smoked turkey leg (if used).
- Season the peas with salt, black pepper, and smoked paprika, if desired. Adjust the seasoning to taste.
- Serve the black-eyed peas hot, garnished with chopped fresh parsley or green onions if desired.
- Offer hot sauce on the side for those who enjoy extra heat.

Enjoy:
- Enjoy the warm and comforting flavor of Southern-style black-eyed peas as a side dish or main course, traditionally served with cornbread, rice, or greens.

This recipe results in tender and flavorful black-eyed peas with a rich, smoky taste, perfect for enjoying as part of a hearty Southern meal. Adjust the seasoning and ingredients according to your taste preferences.

Sweet Potato Pie

Ingredients:

- 1 9-inch unbaked pie crust (homemade or store-bought)
- 2 cups mashed sweet potatoes (about 2 large sweet potatoes)
- 3/4 cup granulated sugar
- 1/2 cup unsalted butter, melted
- 2 large eggs, beaten
- 1/2 cup evaporated milk
- 1 teaspoon vanilla extract
- 1/2 teaspoon ground cinnamon
- 1/4 teaspoon ground nutmeg
- 1/4 teaspoon ground ginger
- 1/4 teaspoon salt

Instructions:

Prepare the Pie Crust:
- Preheat your oven to 350°F (175°C). Place the unbaked pie crust in a 9-inch pie dish and crimp the edges as desired. Set aside.

Cook and Mash the Sweet Potatoes:
- Wash the sweet potatoes and pierce them several times with a fork. Place them on a baking sheet and bake in the preheated oven for 45-60 minutes, or until they are tender when pierced with a fork.
- Remove the sweet potatoes from the oven and let them cool slightly. Peel off the skins and mash the flesh with a fork or potato masher until smooth. Measure out 2 cups of mashed sweet potatoes and set aside.

Make the Filling:
- In a large mixing bowl, combine the mashed sweet potatoes, granulated sugar, melted butter, beaten eggs, evaporated milk, vanilla extract, ground cinnamon, ground nutmeg, ground ginger, and salt. Mix until well combined and smooth.

Assemble and Bake the Pie:
- Pour the sweet potato filling into the prepared pie crust, smoothing the top with a spatula.
- Place the pie in the preheated oven and bake for 55-60 minutes, or until the filling is set and a toothpick inserted into the center comes out clean.
- If the crust starts to brown too quickly, you can cover the edges with aluminum foil halfway through baking.

Cool and Serve:
- Once baked, remove the sweet potato pie from the oven and let it cool completely on a wire rack.

- Once cooled, slice the pie into wedges and serve at room temperature.
- Optionally, serve with whipped cream or vanilla ice cream for an extra treat.

Enjoy:

- Enjoy the rich and comforting flavor of Southern sweet potato pie as a delicious dessert or treat during the holiday season or any time of year.

This classic Southern sweet potato pie is sure to be a hit with friends and family. Adjust the sweetness and spices to suit your taste preferences.

Fried Catfish

Ingredients:

- 4 catfish fillets, about 6-8 ounces each
- 1 cup cornmeal
- 1/2 cup all-purpose flour
- 1 teaspoon salt
- 1/2 teaspoon black pepper
- 1/2 teaspoon paprika
- 1/2 teaspoon garlic powder
- 1/2 teaspoon onion powder
- 1/4 teaspoon cayenne pepper (optional, for heat)
- Vegetable oil, for frying
- Lemon wedges, for serving
- Tartar sauce or hot sauce, for serving (optional)

Instructions:

Prepare the Catfish:
- Rinse the catfish fillets under cold water and pat them dry with paper towels. Cut the fillets into smaller pieces if desired.

Prepare the Breading Mixture:
- In a shallow dish or bowl, mix together the cornmeal, flour, salt, black pepper, paprika, garlic powder, onion powder, and cayenne pepper (if using) until well combined. This will be your breading mixture.

Coat the Catfish:
- Dredge each catfish fillet in the breading mixture, pressing gently to coat both sides evenly. Shake off any excess breading and place the coated fillets on a plate.

Heat the Oil:
- In a large skillet or frying pan, heat enough vegetable oil to cover the bottom of the pan to a temperature of 350°F (175°C) over medium-high heat.

Fry the Catfish:
- Carefully place the breaded catfish fillets in the hot oil, being careful not to overcrowd the pan. Fry in batches if necessary.
- Fry the catfish for about 3-4 minutes on each side, or until golden brown and crispy. Use tongs to carefully flip the fillets halfway through cooking.
- Once cooked, transfer the fried catfish to a plate lined with paper towels to drain excess oil.

Serve:
- Serve the fried catfish hot, garnished with lemon wedges.

- Optionally, serve with tartar sauce or hot sauce on the side for dipping.
- Enjoy the crispy and flavorful goodness of Southern fried catfish as a main dish or as part of a seafood feast!

This recipe yields tender and flaky catfish fillets with a crispy and golden-brown crust, perfect for a Southern-style meal. Adjust the seasoning and level of heat to suit your taste preferences.

Biscuits and Gravy

Ingredients:

- 8 biscuits (homemade or store-bought)
- 1/2 pound breakfast sausage (pork or turkey)
- 2 tablespoons unsalted butter
- 1/4 cup all-purpose flour
- 2 cups whole milk
- Salt and black pepper to taste

Instructions:

Prepare the Biscuits:
- Prepare your biscuits according to your preferred recipe or package instructions. Keep them warm while you prepare the gravy.

Cook the Sausage:
- In a large skillet over medium heat, cook the breakfast sausage, breaking it apart with a spatula, until it's browned and cooked through. Remove the cooked sausage from the skillet, leaving the rendered fat in the pan.

Make the Gravy:
- In the same skillet with the rendered fat, add the butter and let it melt.
- Sprinkle the flour over the melted butter and whisk continuously to form a roux. Cook the roux for about 1-2 minutes until it's golden brown and fragrant.
- Slowly pour in the milk while whisking constantly to prevent lumps from forming. Continue whisking until the mixture thickens and comes to a gentle simmer.

Simmer the Gravy:
- Reduce the heat to low and let the gravy simmer for 5-10 minutes, stirring occasionally, until it reaches your desired thickness.
- Season the gravy with salt and black pepper to taste. Keep in mind that the sausage is already seasoned, so adjust the seasoning accordingly.

Serve:
- To serve, split the warm biscuits in half and place them on serving plates.
- Spoon the warm sausage gravy over the biscuits.
- Serve immediately, and enjoy this classic Southern comfort food dish for breakfast or brunch!

This recipe yields rich and creamy sausage gravy with tender and flaky biscuits, perfect for a hearty and satisfying meal. Feel free to adjust the seasonings and thickness of the gravy according to your preference.

Hush Puppies

Ingredients:

- 1 cup yellow cornmeal
- 1/2 cup all-purpose flour
- 1 teaspoon baking powder
- 1/2 teaspoon baking soda
- 1/2 teaspoon salt
- 1/2 teaspoon onion powder
- 1/2 teaspoon garlic powder
- 1/4 teaspoon black pepper
- 1/4 teaspoon paprika
- 1/2 cup finely chopped onion
- 1/4 cup finely chopped green bell pepper (optional)
- 1 large egg
- 1/2 cup buttermilk
- Vegetable oil, for frying

Instructions:

Prepare the Batter:
- In a large mixing bowl, combine the cornmeal, flour, baking powder, baking soda, salt, onion powder, garlic powder, black pepper, and paprika. Mix well to combine.
- Add the finely chopped onion and green bell pepper (if using) to the dry ingredients and stir until evenly distributed.

Add Wet Ingredients:
- In a separate bowl, beat the egg lightly, then add the buttermilk. Mix until well combined.

Combine Wet and Dry Ingredients:
- Pour the wet ingredients into the dry ingredients and stir until just combined. Do not overmix; a few lumps in the batter are okay.

Fry the Hush Puppies:
- In a deep skillet or Dutch oven, heat vegetable oil to 350°F (175°C) over medium-high heat.
- Using a spoon or cookie scoop, drop spoonfuls of batter into the hot oil, making sure not to overcrowd the skillet. You may need to fry in batches.
- Fry the hush puppies for 2-3 minutes per side, or until they are golden brown and crispy.
- Use a slotted spoon or spider strainer to transfer the fried hush puppies to a plate lined with paper towels to drain excess oil.

Serve:

- Serve the hush puppies hot as a side dish or appetizer.
- Optionally, serve with tartar sauce, remoulade, or hot sauce for dipping.
- Enjoy the crispy and savory goodness of homemade Southern hush puppies!

This recipe yields crispy-on-the-outside and tender-on-the-inside hush puppies with a delicious flavor from the onion and spices. Adjust the seasoning and add-ins according to your taste preferences.

Southern Fried Pork Chops

Ingredients:

- 4 pork chops, bone-in or boneless, about 3/4-inch thick
- 1 cup all-purpose flour
- 1 teaspoon garlic powder
- 1 teaspoon onion powder
- 1 teaspoon paprika
- 1/2 teaspoon salt
- 1/2 teaspoon black pepper
- 2 large eggs
- 2 tablespoons milk or buttermilk
- Vegetable oil, for frying

Instructions:

Prepare the Pork Chops:
- Pat the pork chops dry with paper towels to remove any excess moisture.
- In a shallow dish, combine the flour, garlic powder, onion powder, paprika, salt, and black pepper. Mix well to combine.

Dredge the Pork Chops:
- In another shallow dish, whisk together the eggs and milk or buttermilk until well combined.
- Dip each pork chop into the egg mixture, allowing any excess to drip off.
- Dredge the pork chops in the seasoned flour mixture, pressing gently to coat both sides evenly. Shake off any excess flour.

Heat the Oil:
- In a large skillet or frying pan, heat enough vegetable oil to cover the bottom of the pan to a temperature of 350°F (175°C) over medium-high heat.

Fry the Pork Chops:
- Carefully place the breaded pork chops in the hot oil, being careful not to overcrowd the pan. Fry in batches if necessary.
- Fry the pork chops for 4-5 minutes on each side, or until they are golden brown and cooked through. The internal temperature should reach 145°F (63°C) for medium doneness.
- Use tongs to carefully flip the pork chops halfway through cooking.

Drain and Serve:
- Once cooked, transfer the fried pork chops to a plate lined with paper towels to drain excess oil.
- Let the pork chops rest for a few minutes before serving to allow the juices to redistribute.

Serve:
- Serve the Southern fried pork chops hot as a main dish.
- Optionally, serve with mashed potatoes, gravy, coleslaw, or your favorite Southern sides.
- Enjoy the crispy and flavorful goodness of Southern fried pork chops!

This recipe yields tender and juicy pork chops with a crispy and golden-brown crust, perfect for a classic Southern-style meal. Adjust the seasoning according to your taste preferences.

Red Beans and Rice

Ingredients:

- 1 pound dried red kidney beans
- 8 cups water
- 2 tablespoons vegetable oil
- 1 large onion, diced
- 1 bell pepper, diced
- 3 ribs celery, diced
- 4 cloves garlic, minced
- 1 teaspoon dried thyme
- 1 teaspoon dried oregano
- 1 bay leaf
- 1 teaspoon smoked paprika
- 1/2 teaspoon cayenne pepper (adjust to taste)
- Salt and black pepper to taste
- Cooked white rice, for serving
- Chopped green onions, for garnish (optional)

Instructions:

Prepare the Beans:
- Rinse the dried red kidney beans under cold water and pick out any debris or discolored beans.
- In a large pot, combine the rinsed beans and 8 cups of water. Bring to a boil over high heat, then reduce the heat to low and let the beans simmer, partially covered, for 1.5 to 2 hours, or until they are tender. Stir occasionally and add more water if needed to keep the beans submerged.

Cook the Aromatics:
- In a separate large skillet, heat the vegetable oil over medium heat. Add the diced onion, bell pepper, and celery to the skillet. Cook, stirring occasionally, until the vegetables are softened, about 5-7 minutes.
- Add the minced garlic to the skillet and cook for an additional 1-2 minutes until fragrant.

Combine Ingredients:
- Once the beans are tender, add the cooked vegetables to the pot with the beans.
- Stir in the dried thyme, dried oregano, bay leaf, smoked paprika, and cayenne pepper. Season with salt and black pepper to taste.

Simmer:
- Let the red beans mixture simmer, uncovered, for an additional 30-45 minutes, stirring occasionally, until the flavors are well combined and the mixture thickens to your desired consistency.

Serve:
- Remove the bay leaf from the red beans mixture.
- Serve the red beans over cooked white rice.
- Optionally, garnish with chopped green onions for added flavor and color.
- Enjoy this classic Southern comfort food dish of red beans and rice as a satisfying and flavorful meal!

This recipe yields a hearty and flavorful dish of red beans and rice, perfect for a comforting Southern-style meal. Adjust the seasoning and level of spice according to your taste preferences.

Shrimp and Grits

Ingredients:

- 1 cup stone-ground grits
- 4 cups water or chicken broth
- Salt and black pepper to taste
- 1 pound large shrimp, peeled and deveined
- 2 tablespoons unsalted butter
- 4 slices bacon, chopped
- 1 small onion, finely chopped
- 1 bell pepper, finely chopped
- 2 cloves garlic, minced
- 1 cup cherry tomatoes, halved
- 1/2 cup chicken broth
- 1/4 cup heavy cream
- 2 tablespoons fresh lemon juice
- 2 tablespoons chopped fresh parsley
- Hot sauce, for serving (optional)

Instructions:

Cook the Grits:
- In a medium saucepan, bring the water or chicken broth to a boil. Slowly whisk in the grits and reduce the heat to low.
- Cook the grits according to the package instructions, stirring occasionally, until they are thick and creamy. Season with salt and black pepper to taste.

Prepare the Shrimp:
- Season the shrimp with salt and black pepper to taste.
- In a large skillet, melt 1 tablespoon of butter over medium-high heat. Add the shrimp to the skillet and cook for 2-3 minutes per side, or until they are pink and cooked through. Remove the shrimp from the skillet and set aside.

Cook the Bacon and Vegetables:
- In the same skillet, add the chopped bacon and cook until it becomes crispy. Remove the bacon from the skillet and set aside, leaving the rendered fat in the skillet.

- Add the remaining tablespoon of butter to the skillet. Add the chopped onion and bell pepper to the skillet and cook until they are softened, about 3-4 minutes.
- Stir in the minced garlic and cook for an additional 1-2 minutes until fragrant.
- Add the cherry tomatoes to the skillet and cook for 2-3 minutes until they begin to soften.

Make the Sauce:
- Pour the chicken broth into the skillet and bring to a simmer. Let the mixture simmer for 2-3 minutes.
- Stir in the heavy cream, lemon juice, and chopped parsley. Cook for an additional 1-2 minutes until the sauce thickens slightly.

Combine and Serve:
- Return the cooked shrimp to the skillet and toss them in the sauce to coat.
- Serve the shrimp and vegetable mixture over the cooked grits.
- Garnish with the crispy bacon.
- Optionally, serve with hot sauce on the side for extra heat.

Enjoy:
- Enjoy this flavorful and comforting Southern dish of shrimp and grits as a delicious meal for breakfast, brunch, or dinner!

This recipe yields creamy and flavorful grits topped with tender shrimp and a rich and savory sauce. Adjust the seasoning and level of spice according to your taste preferences.

BBQ Ribs

Ingredients:

- 2 racks of pork baby back ribs
- Salt and black pepper to taste
- 1 cup barbecue sauce (homemade or store-bought)
- 2 tablespoons brown sugar (optional, for extra sweetness)
- 1 tablespoon apple cider vinegar
- 1 teaspoon smoked paprika
- 1/2 teaspoon garlic powder
- 1/2 teaspoon onion powder
- 1/2 teaspoon chili powder (adjust to taste)
- 1/4 teaspoon cayenne pepper (optional, for heat)
- Vegetable oil, for grilling

Instructions:

Prepare the Ribs:
- Remove the membrane from the back of the ribs: Slide a butter knife under the membrane and lift it away from the bone. Grab the membrane with a paper towel and pull it off.

Season the Ribs:
- Season the ribs generously with salt and black pepper on both sides.

Prepare the BBQ Sauce:
- In a small bowl, combine the barbecue sauce, brown sugar (if using), apple cider vinegar, smoked paprika, garlic powder, onion powder, chili powder, and cayenne pepper (if using). Mix well to combine.

Preheat the Grill:
- Preheat your grill to medium-high heat (around 300-325°F or 150-160°C).

Grill the Ribs:
- Brush the grill grates with vegetable oil to prevent sticking.
- Place the seasoned ribs on the grill, bone side down, and cook for 30 minutes, turning occasionally to prevent burning.

Apply the BBQ Sauce:
- After the initial 30 minutes of cooking, brush the ribs with the prepared barbecue sauce, coating them evenly on both sides.
- Continue grilling the ribs for an additional 30-45 minutes, brushing with more barbecue sauce every 10-15 minutes, until the ribs are tender and caramelized. The internal temperature should reach at least 145°F (63°C).

Rest and Serve:

- Once cooked, transfer the ribs to a cutting board and let them rest for a few minutes before slicing.
- Slice the ribs between the bones and serve hot, with extra barbecue sauce on the side if desired.

Enjoy:

- Enjoy these delicious Southern BBQ ribs as a main dish for a backyard barbecue or any occasion!

This recipe yields tender and flavorful BBQ ribs with a smoky, caramelized crust and a rich barbecue sauce glaze. Adjust the seasoning and level of spice in the barbecue sauce according to your taste preferences.

Peach Cobbler

Ingredients:

For the Filling:

- 6 cups fresh or frozen sliced peaches (about 6-8 peaches)
- 1/2 cup granulated sugar
- 1/4 cup brown sugar
- 1 teaspoon vanilla extract
- 1/2 teaspoon ground cinnamon
- 1/4 teaspoon ground nutmeg
- 2 tablespoons cornstarch
- 1 tablespoon lemon juice

For the Cobbler Topping:

- 1 cup all-purpose flour
- 1/2 cup granulated sugar
- 1 teaspoon baking powder
- 1/2 teaspoon salt
- 1/2 cup unsalted butter, melted
- 1/4 cup milk
- Vanilla ice cream or whipped cream, for serving (optional)

Instructions:

Preheat the Oven:
- Preheat your oven to 375°F (190°C). Grease a 9x13-inch baking dish or similar-sized casserole dish with butter or cooking spray.

Prepare the Peach Filling:
- In a large bowl, combine the sliced peaches, granulated sugar, brown sugar, vanilla extract, ground cinnamon, ground nutmeg, cornstarch, and lemon juice. Toss until the peaches are evenly coated. Let the mixture sit while you prepare the cobbler topping.

Make the Cobbler Topping:
- In a separate bowl, whisk together the flour, granulated sugar, baking powder, and salt until well combined.
- Add the melted butter and milk to the dry ingredients and stir until a thick batter forms. It's okay if there are a few lumps.

Assemble the Cobbler:

- Pour the peach filling into the prepared baking dish, spreading it out evenly.
- Drop spoonfuls of the cobbler batter over the top of the peach filling, covering it as evenly as possible.

Bake the Cobbler:
- Place the baking dish in the preheated oven and bake for 35-40 minutes, or until the cobbler topping is golden brown and the peach filling is bubbling around the edges.

Serve:
- Remove the peach cobbler from the oven and let it cool for a few minutes before serving.
- Serve warm, topped with vanilla ice cream or whipped cream if desired.

Enjoy:
- Enjoy the sweet and fruity goodness of Southern peach cobbler as a delightful dessert for any occasion!

This recipe yields a classic Southern peach cobbler with tender peaches and a golden-brown cobbler topping. Adjust the sweetness and spices according to your taste preferences.

Chicken and Waffles

Ingredients:

For the Fried Chicken:

- 4 boneless, skinless chicken breasts or 8 bone-in chicken thighs
- Salt and black pepper to taste
- 1 cup all-purpose flour
- 1 teaspoon garlic powder
- 1 teaspoon onion powder
- 1/2 teaspoon smoked paprika
- 1/2 teaspoon cayenne pepper (adjust to taste)
- 2 large eggs
- 2 tablespoons milk
- Vegetable oil, for frying

For the Waffles:

- 2 cups all-purpose flour
- 2 tablespoons granulated sugar
- 1 tablespoon baking powder
- 1/2 teaspoon salt
- 2 large eggs
- 1 3/4 cups milk
- 1/2 cup unsalted butter, melted
- Non-stick cooking spray or additional melted butter, for greasing the waffle iron

For Serving:

- Maple syrup
- Butter

Instructions:

Prepare the Fried Chicken:
- If using chicken breasts, pound them to an even thickness. Season both sides of the chicken with salt and black pepper.
- In a shallow dish, mix together the flour, garlic powder, onion powder, smoked paprika, and cayenne pepper.

- In another shallow dish, whisk together the eggs and milk until well combined.
- Dip each piece of chicken into the flour mixture, then the egg mixture, and then back into the flour mixture, ensuring each piece is evenly coated.
- Heat vegetable oil in a large skillet or deep fryer to 350°F (175°C). Fry the chicken in batches for about 6-8 minutes per side, or until golden brown and cooked through. Transfer to a wire rack to drain excess oil.

Make the Waffles:
- Preheat your waffle iron according to the manufacturer's instructions.
- In a large mixing bowl, whisk together the flour, sugar, baking powder, and salt.
- In another bowl, beat the eggs, then stir in the milk and melted butter until well combined.
- Pour the wet ingredients into the dry ingredients and stir until just combined. Do not overmix; a few lumps are okay.
- Lightly grease the waffle iron with non-stick cooking spray or melted butter. Pour the batter onto the hot waffle iron and cook according to the manufacturer's instructions until golden brown and crispy.

Assemble and Serve:
- Place a cooked waffle on a plate, then top with fried chicken pieces.
- Drizzle with maple syrup and add a pat of butter on top.
- Serve immediately and enjoy the delicious combination of crispy fried chicken and fluffy waffles!

This recipe yields a classic Southern dish of chicken and waffles, perfect for a special breakfast or brunch. Adjust the seasoning and level of spice according to your taste preferences.

Candied Yams

Ingredients:

- 4 medium sweet potatoes or yams
- 1/2 cup unsalted butter, melted
- 1 cup brown sugar
- 1/2 teaspoon ground cinnamon
- 1/4 teaspoon ground nutmeg
- 1/4 teaspoon salt
- 1 teaspoon vanilla extract
- Mini marshmallows (optional, for topping)

Instructions:

Preheat the Oven:
- Preheat your oven to 350°F (175°C). Grease a 9x13-inch baking dish with butter or cooking spray.

Prepare the Sweet Potatoes:
- Peel the sweet potatoes and cut them into slices or cubes, about 1/4 to 1/2 inch thick.

Make the Candied Yams:
- In a large bowl, combine the melted butter, brown sugar, ground cinnamon, ground nutmeg, salt, and vanilla extract. Mix until well combined.
- Add the sweet potato slices or cubes to the bowl and toss until they are evenly coated with the sugar mixture.

Bake:
- Transfer the coated sweet potatoes to the prepared baking dish, spreading them out in an even layer.
- Cover the baking dish with aluminum foil and bake in the preheated oven for 45 minutes to 1 hour, or until the sweet potatoes are tender when pierced with a fork.

Add Marshmallows (Optional):
- If desired, remove the foil from the baking dish and sprinkle mini marshmallows over the top of the candied yams.
- Return the baking dish to the oven and bake for an additional 5-10 minutes, or until the marshmallows are golden brown and bubbly.

Serve:
- Remove the candied yams from the oven and let them cool for a few minutes before serving.
- Serve warm as a side dish or dessert for a delicious taste of Southern comfort food.

This recipe yields sweet and tender candied yams with a caramelized brown sugar glaze, perfect for serving alongside your favorite holiday meals or as a comforting treat any time of year. Adjust the sweetness and spices according to your taste preferences.

Banana Pudding

Ingredients:

- 4 large ripe bananas, sliced
- 1 box (11 oz) vanilla wafers
- 2/3 cup granulated sugar
- 1/4 cup all-purpose flour
- 1/4 teaspoon salt
- 4 large egg yolks
- 2 cups whole milk
- 1 teaspoon vanilla extract
- 1 tablespoon unsalted butter
- Whipped cream, for topping
- Additional banana slices and vanilla wafers, for garnish (optional)

Instructions:

Layer the Pudding:
- In a large bowl or trifle dish, layer the sliced bananas and vanilla wafers, creating alternating layers until all the bananas and wafers are used. Set aside.

Make the Pudding Custard:
- In a medium saucepan, whisk together the granulated sugar, flour, and salt.
- In a separate bowl, whisk the egg yolks until smooth. Gradually whisk in the milk until well combined.
- Gradually pour the egg mixture into the saucepan with the dry ingredients, whisking constantly until smooth.
- Place the saucepan over medium heat and cook, stirring constantly, until the mixture thickens and comes to a gentle boil, about 8-10 minutes.
- Remove the saucepan from the heat and stir in the vanilla extract and unsalted butter until the butter is melted and the mixture is smooth.

Assemble the Pudding:
- Pour the hot custard over the layered bananas and vanilla wafers in the bowl or trifle dish, ensuring that the custard evenly coats the layers.
- Gently tap the dish on the countertop to allow the custard to settle into the layers.

- Let the pudding cool to room temperature, then cover and refrigerate for at least 4 hours or overnight to allow the flavors to meld and the pudding to set.

Serve:
- Before serving, top the chilled banana pudding with whipped cream.
- Garnish with additional banana slices and vanilla wafers, if desired.
- Serve cold and enjoy the creamy and delicious Southern banana pudding!

This recipe yields a classic Southern banana pudding with layers of ripe bananas, vanilla wafers, and creamy custard, topped with whipped cream for a delightful dessert that's perfect for any occasion. Adjust the sweetness and thickness of the custard according to your taste preferences.

Buttermilk Biscuits

Ingredients:

- 2 cups all-purpose flour, plus more for dusting
- 1 tablespoon baking powder
- 1 teaspoon granulated sugar
- 1/2 teaspoon salt
- 1/2 cup unsalted butter, cold and cubed
- 3/4 cup buttermilk, cold

Instructions:

Preheat the Oven:
- Preheat your oven to 425°F (220°C). Line a baking sheet with parchment paper or lightly grease it with butter.

Prepare the Dry Ingredients:
- In a large mixing bowl, whisk together the all-purpose flour, baking powder, granulated sugar, and salt until well combined.

Cut in the Butter:
- Add the cold, cubed butter to the dry ingredients. Using a pastry cutter or two knives, cut the butter into the flour mixture until it resembles coarse crumbs. You can also use your fingertips to rub the butter into the flour.

Add the Buttermilk:
- Make a well in the center of the flour mixture and pour in the cold buttermilk.
- Use a spatula or wooden spoon to gently stir the mixture until the dough comes together. Be careful not to overmix; the dough should be shaggy and slightly sticky.

Shape the Biscuits:
- Turn the dough out onto a lightly floured surface. Use your hands to gently pat the dough into a rectangle, about 1/2 to 3/4 inch thick.
- Use a floured biscuit cutter or the rim of a glass to cut out biscuits from the dough. Press straight down and avoid twisting the cutter to ensure the biscuits rise evenly.
- Gather any remaining dough scraps and gently pat them together to cut out more biscuits.

Bake the Biscuits:
- Place the cut biscuits onto the prepared baking sheet, leaving a little space between each biscuit for expansion.
- Bake in the preheated oven for 12-15 minutes, or until the biscuits are golden brown on top and cooked through.

Serve:

- Remove the biscuits from the oven and let them cool slightly on the baking sheet for a few minutes.
- Serve the warm buttermilk biscuits with butter, jam, gravy, or your favorite toppings.

Enjoy:
- Enjoy these homemade Southern buttermilk biscuits as a delicious addition to breakfast, brunch, or any meal!

This recipe yields tender and flaky buttermilk biscuits with a golden-brown crust, perfect for serving alongside your favorite dishes or as a base for sandwiches. Adjust the thickness of the dough and baking time according to your preference for thicker or thinner biscuits.

Okra Gumbo

Ingredients:

- 1/2 cup vegetable oil
- 1/2 cup all-purpose flour
- 1 large onion, diced
- 1 bell pepper, diced
- 2 ribs celery, diced
- 3 cloves garlic, minced
- 1 pound okra, sliced
- 1 can (14.5 oz) diced tomatoes
- 6 cups chicken or vegetable broth
- 1 pound Andouille sausage, sliced
- 1 teaspoon dried thyme
- 1 teaspoon dried oregano
- 1/2 teaspoon paprika
- 1/4 teaspoon cayenne pepper (adjust to taste)
- Salt and black pepper to taste
- Cooked rice, for serving
- Chopped green onions, for garnish
- File powder (optional, for serving)

Instructions:

Prepare the Roux:
- In a large Dutch oven or heavy-bottomed pot, heat the vegetable oil over medium heat. Gradually add the flour, stirring constantly to combine.
- Cook the flour and oil mixture, stirring frequently, until it turns a dark caramel color, similar to peanut butter. This process can take about 20-30 minutes. Be careful not to burn the roux.

Saute the Aromatics:
- Once the roux reaches the desired color, add the diced onion, bell pepper, celery, and minced garlic to the pot. Stir to coat the vegetables in the roux.
- Cook the vegetables, stirring occasionally, until they are softened, about 5-7 minutes.

Add the Okra and Tomatoes:
- Add the sliced okra to the pot and cook for an additional 5 minutes, stirring occasionally.
- Stir in the diced tomatoes (with their juices) and cook for another 5 minutes.

Make the Gumbo Base:

- Gradually pour in the chicken or vegetable broth, stirring constantly to incorporate it into the roux and vegetable mixture.
- Add the sliced Andouille sausage, dried thyme, dried oregano, paprika, and cayenne pepper to the pot. Season with salt and black pepper to taste.
- Bring the gumbo to a simmer, then reduce the heat to low. Cover and let it simmer gently for about 1 hour, stirring occasionally.

Serve:
- Once the gumbo has thickened and the flavors have melded together, taste and adjust the seasoning if necessary.
- Serve the okra gumbo hot over cooked rice.
- Garnish each serving with chopped green onions and a sprinkle of file powder, if desired.

Enjoy:
- Enjoy the rich and flavorful Southern okra gumbo as a comforting meal on its own or as part of a traditional Cajun feast!

This recipe yields a hearty and satisfying okra gumbo with a thick and flavorful broth, perfect for warming up on a chilly day or serving at a festive gathering. Adjust the seasoning and level of spice according to your taste preferences.

Crawfish Étouffée

Ingredients:

- 1/2 cup unsalted butter
- 1/2 cup all-purpose flour
- 1 large onion, finely chopped
- 1 bell pepper, finely chopped
- 2 ribs celery, finely chopped
- 3 cloves garlic, minced
- 2 cups seafood or chicken broth
- 1 can (14.5 oz) diced tomatoes
- 2 tablespoons tomato paste
- 1 teaspoon paprika
- 1/2 teaspoon dried thyme
- 1/2 teaspoon dried oregano
- 1/4 teaspoon cayenne pepper (adjust to taste)
- Salt and black pepper to taste
- 2 pounds crawfish tails, peeled and deveined
- 1/4 cup chopped fresh parsley
- Cooked rice, for serving
- Chopped green onions, for garnish

Instructions:

Make the Roux:
- In a large Dutch oven or heavy-bottomed pot, melt the unsalted butter over medium heat.
- Gradually whisk in the all-purpose flour to form a roux. Cook the roux, stirring constantly, until it turns a golden caramel color, about 10-15 minutes.

Saute the Aromatics:
- Add the chopped onion, bell pepper, celery, and minced garlic to the roux. Cook, stirring occasionally, until the vegetables are softened, about 5-7 minutes.

Prepare the Sauce:
- Gradually pour in the seafood or chicken broth, stirring constantly to incorporate it into the roux and vegetable mixture.
- Stir in the diced tomatoes (with their juices), tomato paste, paprika, dried thyme, dried oregano, and cayenne pepper. Season with salt and black pepper to taste.

Simmer the Étouffée:
- Bring the mixture to a simmer, then reduce the heat to low. Cover and let it simmer gently for about 20-30 minutes, stirring occasionally, to allow the flavors to meld together and the sauce to thicken.

Add the Crawfish:
- Once the sauce has thickened to your desired consistency, add the peeled and deveined crawfish tails to the pot.
- Cook for an additional 5-7 minutes, or until the crawfish tails are heated through and cooked.

Finish and Serve:
- Stir in the chopped fresh parsley, then taste and adjust the seasoning if necessary.
- Serve the crawfish étouffée hot over cooked rice.
- Garnish each serving with chopped green onions.

Enjoy:
- Enjoy the rich and flavorful Southern crawfish étouffée as a comforting and satisfying meal, perfect for any occasion!

This recipe yields a delicious and traditional crawfish étouffée with a flavorful sauce that's perfect for serving over hot cooked rice. Adjust the seasoning and level of spice according to your taste preferences.

Jambalaya

Ingredients:

- 1 pound Andouille sausage, sliced
- 1 pound boneless, skinless chicken thighs, cut into bite-sized pieces
- 1 tablespoon vegetable oil
- 1 large onion, diced
- 1 bell pepper, diced
- 2 ribs celery, diced
- 3 cloves garlic, minced
- 1 can (14.5 oz) diced tomatoes
- 3 cups chicken broth
- 1 cup long-grain white rice
- 1 teaspoon paprika
- 1/2 teaspoon dried thyme
- 1/2 teaspoon dried oregano
- 1/4 teaspoon cayenne pepper (adjust to taste)
- Salt and black pepper to taste
- 1 pound medium shrimp, peeled and deveined
- Chopped fresh parsley, for garnish
- Sliced green onions, for garnish

Instructions:

Brown the Sausage and Chicken:
- Heat the vegetable oil in a large Dutch oven or heavy-bottomed pot over medium-high heat.
- Add the sliced Andouille sausage to the pot and cook until it starts to brown, about 3-4 minutes.
- Add the chicken pieces to the pot and cook until browned on all sides, about 5-6 minutes. Remove the sausage and chicken from the pot and set aside.

Saute the Aromatics:
- In the same pot, add the diced onion, bell pepper, and celery. Cook, stirring occasionally, until the vegetables are softened, about 5-7 minutes.
- Add the minced garlic to the pot and cook for an additional 1-2 minutes until fragrant.

Add the Tomatoes and Broth:
- Stir in the diced tomatoes (with their juices) and chicken broth.
- Add the paprika, dried thyme, dried oregano, cayenne pepper, salt, and black pepper to the pot. Stir to combine.

Simmer the Jambalaya:
- Bring the mixture to a boil, then reduce the heat to low. Cover and let it simmer gently for about 10 minutes to allow the flavors to meld together.

Add the Rice and Protein:
- Stir in the uncooked rice, then return the browned sausage and chicken to the pot. Stir to combine.
- Cover and simmer for an additional 20-25 minutes, or until the rice is cooked and the liquid has been absorbed.

Add the Shrimp:
- Once the rice is cooked, add the peeled and deveined shrimp to the pot.
- Cover and cook for an additional 5-7 minutes, or until the shrimp are pink and cooked through.

Finish and Serve:
- Taste and adjust the seasoning if necessary.
- Garnish the jambalaya with chopped fresh parsley and sliced green onions before serving.

Enjoy:
- Serve the jambalaya hot as a flavorful and satisfying meal, perfect for any occasion!

This recipe yields a delicious and authentic jambalaya with a rich combination of flavors from the Andouille sausage, chicken, shrimp, and aromatic vegetables. Adjust the level of spice according to your taste preferences.

Southern Fried Green Tomatoes

Ingredients:

- 4 large green tomatoes, sliced into 1/4-inch rounds
- 1 cup buttermilk
- 1 cup all-purpose flour
- 1 cup cornmeal
- 1 teaspoon salt
- 1/2 teaspoon black pepper
- 1/2 teaspoon paprika
- Vegetable oil, for frying

Instructions:

Prepare the Tomatoes:
- Slice the green tomatoes into 1/4-inch rounds. Discard the ends.
- Place the tomato slices on a paper towel-lined baking sheet to absorb excess moisture.

Soak in Buttermilk:
- Pour the buttermilk into a shallow dish.
- Dip each tomato slice into the buttermilk, coating both sides. Allow any excess buttermilk to drip off.

Prepare the Coating:
- In another shallow dish, combine the all-purpose flour, cornmeal, salt, black pepper, and paprika. Mix well to combine.

Coat the Tomatoes:
- Dip each buttermilk-coated tomato slice into the flour-cornmeal mixture, ensuring that both sides are evenly coated. Press gently to adhere the coating.

Fry the Tomatoes:
- In a large skillet or frying pan, heat enough vegetable oil to cover the bottom of the pan to about 1/4 inch.
- Once the oil is hot, carefully place the coated tomato slices into the hot oil in a single layer, making sure not to overcrowd the pan.
- Fry the tomatoes in batches for about 3-4 minutes on each side, or until golden brown and crispy.
- Use a slotted spoon or tongs to transfer the fried green tomatoes to a paper towel-lined plate to drain excess oil.

Serve:
- Serve the fried green tomatoes hot as a delicious appetizer or side dish.
- Optionally, sprinkle with a little extra salt while still hot for added flavor.

Enjoy:

- Enjoy the crispy and flavorful Southern fried green tomatoes as a classic Southern delicacy!

This recipe yields crispy and flavorful fried green tomatoes with a golden-brown cornmeal coating, perfect for serving as an appetizer, snack, or side dish. Adjust the seasoning according to your taste preferences.

Cornbread Dressing

Ingredients:

- 1 batch of cornbread (about 8 cups crumbled)*
- 6 tablespoons unsalted butter
- 1 large onion, diced
- 4 ribs celery, diced
- 4 cloves garlic, minced
- 1 teaspoon dried sage
- 1 teaspoon dried thyme
- 1/2 teaspoon dried rosemary
- 1/2 teaspoon dried marjoram
- Salt and black pepper to taste
- 4 cups chicken or vegetable broth
- 2 large eggs, beaten
- Chopped fresh parsley, for garnish (optional)

Instructions:

Prepare the Cornbread:
- Bake a batch of cornbread according to your favorite recipe or package instructions. Allow the cornbread to cool completely, then crumble it into a large mixing bowl. You should have about 8 cups of crumbled cornbread.

Saute the Aromatics:
- Preheat your oven to 350°F (175°C).
- In a large skillet or frying pan, melt the unsalted butter over medium heat.
- Add the diced onion and celery to the skillet and cook until softened, about 5-7 minutes.
- Add the minced garlic, dried sage, dried thyme, dried rosemary, and dried marjoram to the skillet. Cook for an additional 1-2 minutes until fragrant. Season with salt and black pepper to taste.

Mix the Dressing:
- Transfer the sautéed aromatics to the bowl with the crumbled cornbread. Mix until well combined.

Moisten the Dressing:
- Gradually pour the chicken or vegetable broth over the cornbread mixture, stirring well to combine. The mixture should be moistened but not overly soggy.
- Taste and adjust the seasoning if necessary.

Add Eggs:
- Stir in the beaten eggs until evenly distributed throughout the dressing mixture. This will help bind the dressing together during baking.

Bake the Dressing:
- Transfer the dressing mixture to a greased 9x13-inch baking dish or a similar-sized casserole dish, spreading it out evenly.
- Cover the dish with aluminum foil and bake in the preheated oven for 30 minutes.
- Remove the foil and continue baking for an additional 15-20 minutes, or until the top is golden brown and crispy.

Serve:
- Remove the cornbread dressing from the oven and let it cool for a few minutes before serving.
- Garnish with chopped fresh parsley, if desired, before serving.

Enjoy:
- Serve the Southern cornbread dressing hot as a delicious side dish for Thanksgiving, Christmas, or any festive meal!

*Note: You can use store-bought cornbread or make your own from scratch for this recipe. Adjust the seasoning and add-ins according to your taste preferences.

Fried Okra

Ingredients:

- 1 pound fresh okra
- 1 cup buttermilk
- 1 cup all-purpose flour
- 1 cup cornmeal
- 1 teaspoon salt
- 1/2 teaspoon black pepper
- 1/2 teaspoon paprika
- Vegetable oil, for frying

Instructions:

Prepare the Okra:
- Wash the okra and trim off the stem ends. Slice the okra into 1/2-inch rounds.

Soak in Buttermilk:
- Place the sliced okra in a bowl and pour the buttermilk over it. Stir to ensure all the okra pieces are coated in buttermilk. Let the okra soak in the buttermilk for about 10-15 minutes.

Prepare the Coating:
- In a separate shallow dish, combine the all-purpose flour, cornmeal, salt, black pepper, and paprika. Mix well to combine.

Coat the Okra:
- Heat vegetable oil in a deep fryer or large skillet to 350°F (175°C).
- Take a handful of the soaked okra slices and dredge them in the flour-cornmeal mixture, coating them evenly. Shake off any excess coating and place the coated okra on a plate. Repeat until all the okra slices are coated.

Fry the Okra:
- Carefully place the coated okra slices into the hot oil in batches, making sure not to overcrowd the fryer or skillet.
- Fry the okra for about 3-4 minutes, or until golden brown and crispy, stirring occasionally to ensure even cooking.
- Use a slotted spoon or tongs to transfer the fried okra to a paper towel-lined plate to drain excess oil. Repeat until all the okra slices are fried.

Serve:
- Serve the fried okra hot as a delicious side dish or appetizer.
- Optionally, sprinkle with a little extra salt while still hot for added flavor.

Enjoy:
- Enjoy the crispy and flavorful Southern fried okra as a classic Southern delicacy!

This recipe yields crispy and flavorful fried okra with a golden-brown cornmeal coating, perfect for serving as a side dish, appetizer, or snack. Adjust the seasoning according to your taste preferences.

Collard Greens with Ham Hocks

Ingredients:

- 2 pounds collard greens, washed and chopped
- 2 smoked ham hocks
- 1 large onion, diced
- 4 cloves garlic, minced
- 4 cups chicken broth or water
- 1 tablespoon apple cider vinegar
- 1 teaspoon sugar
- 1 teaspoon salt, plus more to taste
- 1/2 teaspoon black pepper, plus more to taste
- Pinch of red pepper flakes (optional)
- Hot sauce, for serving (optional)

Instructions:

Prepare the Ham Hocks:
- Rinse the smoked ham hocks under cold water to remove any excess salt. Pat them dry with paper towels.

Cook the Ham Hocks:
- In a large pot or Dutch oven, place the ham hocks and cover them with chicken broth or water.
- Bring the liquid to a boil over medium-high heat, then reduce the heat to low and let the ham hocks simmer, covered, for about 1 hour, or until they are tender and the meat is starting to fall off the bones.

Prepare the Collard Greens:
- While the ham hocks are simmering, wash the collard greens thoroughly under cold water to remove any dirt or grit. Remove the tough stems and chop the leaves into bite-sized pieces.

Saute the Aromatics:
- In a separate skillet, heat a little oil over medium heat. Add the diced onion and minced garlic to the skillet and sauté until softened and fragrant, about 5-7 minutes.

Add the Greens to the Pot:
- Once the ham hocks are tender, add the chopped collard greens to the pot.
- Stir in the sautéed onions and garlic.

Season and Simmer:
- Add the apple cider vinegar, sugar, salt, black pepper, and pinch of red pepper flakes (if using) to the pot.
- Stir well to combine.

- Cover the pot and let the collard greens simmer over low heat for about 1 to 1.5 hours, stirring occasionally, or until the greens are tender and flavorful.

Serve:
- Once the collard greens are tender and cooked to your liking, remove the ham hocks from the pot.
- Use a fork to shred the meat from the bones, discarding any excess fat or skin.
- Return the shredded meat to the pot and stir to combine with the collard greens.
- Taste and adjust the seasoning with additional salt and black pepper, if needed.

Enjoy:
- Serve the Southern collard greens with ham hocks hot as a delicious and comforting side dish.
- Optionally, serve with hot sauce on the side for added heat.

This recipe yields tender and flavorful collard greens with smoky ham hocks, perfect for serving alongside your favorite Southern meals. Adjust the seasoning and level of spice according to your taste preferences.

Pulled Pork Sandwiches

Ingredients:

- 3-4 pounds pork shoulder (also known as pork butt)
- 2 tablespoons brown sugar
- 2 tablespoons paprika
- 1 tablespoon garlic powder
- 1 tablespoon onion powder
- 1 tablespoon chili powder
- 1 tablespoon ground cumin
- 1 tablespoon ground mustard
- 1 tablespoon salt
- 1 teaspoon black pepper
- 1 cup barbecue sauce
- Hamburger buns or sandwich rolls
- Coleslaw, for topping (optional)

Instructions:

Prepare the Pork Shoulder:
- In a small bowl, mix together the brown sugar, paprika, garlic powder, onion powder, chili powder, ground cumin, ground mustard, salt, and black pepper to create a dry rub.
- Rub the dry rub all over the pork shoulder, covering it evenly. Allow the pork shoulder to marinate in the dry rub for at least 1 hour, or preferably overnight in the refrigerator.

Cook the Pork Shoulder:
- Preheat your oven to 325°F (160°C).
- Place the seasoned pork shoulder in a roasting pan or baking dish. Cover tightly with aluminum foil.
- Roast the pork shoulder in the preheated oven for about 4-5 hours, or until the meat is tender and easily shreds with a fork.
- Alternatively, you can cook the pork shoulder in a slow cooker on low heat for 8-10 hours, or until tender.

Shred the Pork:
- Once the pork shoulder is cooked and tender, remove it from the oven or slow cooker.
- Use two forks to shred the pork into bite-sized pieces, discarding any excess fat or bone.
- Place the shredded pork in a large bowl.

Add Barbecue Sauce:

- Pour the barbecue sauce over the shredded pork and toss until the pork is evenly coated in sauce.
- If you prefer a saucier sandwich, you can add more barbecue sauce to taste.

Assemble the Sandwiches:
- Toast the hamburger buns or sandwich rolls, if desired.
- Spoon the saucy pulled pork onto the bottom half of each bun.
- Top with coleslaw, if using, and cover with the top half of the bun.

Serve:
- Serve the Southern pulled pork sandwiches hot as a delicious and satisfying meal.

Enjoy:
- Enjoy the tender and flavorful pulled pork sandwiches as a classic Southern favorite, perfect for any occasion!

This recipe yields delicious and juicy pulled pork sandwiches with a smoky and savory flavor, perfect for serving at backyard barbecues, parties, or family gatherings. Adjust the seasoning and barbecue sauce according to your taste preferences.

Fried Catfish Po' Boy

Ingredients:

For the Fried Catfish:

- 4 catfish fillets, about 6-8 ounces each
- 1 cup cornmeal
- 1/2 cup all-purpose flour
- 1 tablespoon Cajun seasoning (or to taste)
- Salt and black pepper to taste
- Vegetable oil for frying

For the Po' Boy:

- 4 soft French bread rolls (or baguette)
- 1 cup shredded lettuce
- 1 large tomato, sliced
- Sliced pickles (optional)
- Remoulade sauce or tartar sauce
- Lemon wedges for serving

Instructions:

Prepare the Catfish:
- In a shallow dish, mix together the cornmeal, all-purpose flour, Cajun seasoning, salt, and black pepper.
- Pat the catfish fillets dry with paper towels, then dredge them in the cornmeal mixture, coating both sides evenly.

Fry the Catfish:
- In a large skillet or frying pan, heat about 1/2 inch of vegetable oil over medium-high heat until hot but not smoking.
- Carefully add the coated catfish fillets to the hot oil, working in batches if necessary to avoid overcrowding the pan.
- Fry the catfish fillets for about 3-4 minutes on each side, or until golden brown and crispy. Use tongs to carefully flip them halfway through cooking.
- Once cooked, transfer the fried catfish fillets to a paper towel-lined plate to drain any excess oil.

Assemble the Po' Boys:

- Slice the French bread rolls or baguette horizontally, but not all the way through, creating a pocket for the fillings.
- Spread remoulade sauce or tartar sauce on both sides of the bread.
- Layer shredded lettuce on the bottom half of each roll.
- Place a fried catfish fillet on top of the lettuce.
- Add sliced tomato and pickles, if desired.
- Close the sandwiches with the top halves of the rolls.

Serve:
- Serve the fried catfish po' boys immediately, accompanied by lemon wedges for squeezing over the fish.
- Optionally, serve with additional remoulade sauce or tartar sauce on the side for dipping.

Enjoy:
- Enjoy these delicious Southern fried catfish po' boys as a satisfying and flavorful meal!

This recipe yields crispy and golden-brown fried catfish fillets served in soft French bread rolls with classic po' boy toppings, creating a mouthwatering sandwich that's perfect for lunch or dinner. Adjust the seasoning and toppings according to your taste preferences.

Smothered Pork Chops

Ingredients:

- 4 pork chops, bone-in or boneless (about 1 inch thick)
- Salt and black pepper to taste
- 1/2 cup all-purpose flour
- 2 tablespoons vegetable oil or bacon grease
- 1 large onion, thinly sliced
- 2 cloves garlic, minced
- 2 cups chicken broth or beef broth
- 1 teaspoon Worcestershire sauce
- 1/2 teaspoon dried thyme
- 1/2 teaspoon dried rosemary
- 1/2 teaspoon dried sage
- 1/4 teaspoon paprika
- 1/4 teaspoon cayenne pepper (optional)
- Chopped fresh parsley, for garnish (optional)

Instructions:

Season and Coat the Pork Chops:
- Season both sides of the pork chops with salt and black pepper to taste.
- Dredge the seasoned pork chops in the all-purpose flour, shaking off any excess flour. Set aside.

Brown the Pork Chops:
- In a large skillet or frying pan, heat the vegetable oil or bacon grease over medium-high heat.
- Once hot, add the pork chops to the skillet in a single layer, making sure not to overcrowd the pan. Brown the pork chops for about 3-4 minutes on each side, or until golden brown. Remove the browned pork chops from the skillet and set aside.

Saute the Onions and Garlic:
- In the same skillet, add the thinly sliced onion and minced garlic. Cook, stirring occasionally, until the onions are softened and translucent, about 5-7 minutes.

Make the Gravy:
- Sprinkle any remaining flour from dredging the pork chops into the skillet with the onions and garlic. Stir to combine and cook for 1-2 minutes to form a roux.
- Gradually pour in the chicken broth or beef broth, stirring constantly to prevent lumps from forming.
- Stir in the Worcestershire sauce, dried thyme, dried rosemary, dried sage, paprika, and cayenne pepper (if using).

- Bring the mixture to a simmer, then reduce the heat to low.

Simmer the Pork Chops:
- Return the browned pork chops to the skillet, nestling them into the gravy.
- Cover the skillet with a lid and let the pork chops simmer in the gravy over low heat for about 30-40 minutes, or until the pork chops are tender and cooked through, stirring occasionally.

Serve:
- Once the pork chops are cooked to your liking and the gravy has thickened, remove them from the skillet.
- Serve the smothered pork chops hot, spooning the onion gravy over the top.
- Garnish with chopped fresh parsley, if desired.

Enjoy:
- Enjoy these tender and flavorful Southern smothered pork chops as a comforting and satisfying meal, perfect for any occasion!

This recipe yields juicy and tender pork chops smothered in a rich and savory onion gravy, creating a deliciously comforting dish that pairs perfectly with mashed potatoes, rice, or your favorite side dishes. Adjust the seasoning and level of spice according to your taste preferences.

Southern Style Green Beans

Ingredients:

- 1 pound fresh green beans, trimmed
- 4 slices bacon, chopped
- 1 small onion, diced
- 2 cloves garlic, minced
- 2 cups chicken broth or vegetable broth
- 1 teaspoon sugar
- Salt and black pepper to taste

Instructions:

Prepare the Green Beans:
- Wash the green beans under cold water and trim off the ends. Cut the beans into bite-sized pieces, if desired.

Cook the Bacon:
- In a large skillet or Dutch oven, cook the chopped bacon over medium heat until it becomes crispy and golden brown, stirring occasionally.

Saute the Aromatics:
- Add the diced onion to the skillet with the bacon and cook until it becomes translucent, about 3-4 minutes.
- Add the minced garlic to the skillet and cook for an additional 1-2 minutes, until fragrant.

Add the Green Beans:
- Add the trimmed green beans to the skillet with the cooked bacon, onion, and garlic.

Simmer the Green Beans:
- Pour the chicken broth or vegetable broth over the green beans in the skillet.
- Stir in the sugar, salt, and black pepper to taste.

Cook the Green Beans:
- Bring the mixture to a boil, then reduce the heat to low.
- Cover the skillet with a lid and let the green beans simmer for about 20-25 minutes, or until they are tender but still have a slight crunch.

Serve:
- Once the green beans are cooked to your desired tenderness, remove the skillet from the heat.
- Using a slotted spoon, transfer the green beans to a serving dish, leaving the liquid in the skillet.
- Optionally, you can sprinkle some of the cooked bacon and onions over the top of the green beans for extra flavor.

Enjoy:
- Serve the Southern style green beans hot as a delicious and nutritious side dish, perfect for any Southern meal

This recipe yields tender yet slightly crunchy green beans infused with the savory flavor of bacon, onions, and garlic, creating a classic Southern side dish that pairs well with any main course. Adjust the seasoning according to your taste preferences.

Blackened Catfish

Ingredients:

- 4 catfish fillets, about 6-8 ounces each
- 4 tablespoons unsalted butter, melted
- 2 tablespoons paprika
- 1 tablespoon garlic powder
- 1 tablespoon onion powder
- 1 teaspoon dried thyme
- 1 teaspoon dried oregano
- 1 teaspoon cayenne pepper (adjust to taste)
- 1 teaspoon black pepper
- 1 teaspoon salt
- 1 lemon, cut into wedges
- Vegetable oil, for cooking

Instructions:

Prepare the Blackening Seasoning:
- In a small bowl, combine the paprika, garlic powder, onion powder, dried thyme, dried oregano, cayenne pepper, black pepper, and salt. Mix well to create the blackening seasoning.

Prepare the Catfish:
- Pat the catfish fillets dry with paper towels.
- Brush both sides of each catfish fillet with melted butter.

Coat with Blackening Seasoning:
- Generously sprinkle the blackening seasoning over both sides of each catfish fillet, pressing it into the flesh to adhere.

Heat the Skillet:
- Heat a cast-iron skillet or heavy-bottomed skillet over high heat until it's smoking hot.

Cook the Catfish:
- Drizzle a little vegetable oil into the hot skillet, swirling to coat the bottom.
- Carefully add the seasoned catfish fillets to the skillet.
- Cook the catfish fillets for about 3-4 minutes on each side, or until they are blackened and cooked through. The cooking time will depend on the thickness of the fillets.

Serve:
- Once the catfish is cooked through, remove it from the skillet and transfer it to a serving platter.

Garnish and Serve:
- Squeeze fresh lemon juice over the blackened catfish fillets.
- Garnish with additional lemon wedges.
- Serve the blackened catfish hot as a delicious and flavorful main dish.

Enjoy:
- Enjoy the tender and flavorful blackened catfish with its bold seasoning and smoky flavor, perfect for a Southern-inspired meal!

This recipe yields tender and juicy catfish fillets with a crispy and flavorful blackened crust, making it a perfect dish for seafood lovers. Adjust the amount of cayenne pepper according to your desired level of spiciness. Serve the blackened catfish with your favorite side dishes, such as rice, vegetables, or salad, for a complete meal.

Baked Macaroni and Cheese

Ingredients:

- 8 ounces elbow macaroni (or pasta of your choice)
- 4 tablespoons unsalted butter
- 1/4 cup all-purpose flour
- 2 cups milk
- 2 cups shredded cheese (such as cheddar, mozzarella, or a combination)
- 1/2 teaspoon salt
- 1/4 teaspoon black pepper
- 1/4 teaspoon paprika (optional)
- 1/4 teaspoon garlic powder (optional)
- 1/4 cup breadcrumbs (optional)
- Chopped fresh parsley, for garnish (optional)

Instructions:

Preheat the Oven:
- Preheat your oven to 350°F (175°C). Grease a baking dish with butter or cooking spray.

Cook the Pasta:
- Cook the elbow macaroni according to the package instructions until it's al dente. Drain and set aside.

Make the Cheese Sauce:
- In a large saucepan, melt the unsalted butter over medium heat.
- Stir in the all-purpose flour and cook, stirring constantly, for about 1-2 minutes to make a roux.
- Gradually whisk in the milk until the mixture is smooth and well combined.
- Cook the sauce, stirring constantly, until it thickens, about 5-7 minutes.
- Stir in the shredded cheese, salt, black pepper, paprika, and garlic powder (if using). Stir until the cheese is melted and the sauce is smooth and creamy.

Combine Pasta and Cheese Sauce:
- Add the cooked elbow macaroni to the cheese sauce in the saucepan. Stir until the pasta is evenly coated with the cheese sauce.

Transfer to Baking Dish:
- Pour the macaroni and cheese mixture into the greased baking dish, spreading it out evenly.

Optional Toppings:
- If desired, sprinkle breadcrumbs evenly over the top of the macaroni and cheese for a crispy topping.

Bake:
- Bake the macaroni and cheese in the preheated oven for about 25-30 minutes, or until bubbly and golden brown on top.

Garnish and Serve:
- Once baked, remove the macaroni and cheese from the oven.
- Garnish with chopped fresh parsley, if desired.
- Let it cool slightly before serving.

Enjoy:
- Serve the baked macaroni and cheese hot as a delicious and comforting side dish or main course.

This recipe yields creamy and cheesy baked macaroni and cheese with a golden-brown crust on top, making it a classic comfort food dish that's perfect for family dinners, potlucks, or any occasion. Feel free to customize the cheese blend and add extra seasonings or toppings according to your taste preferences.

Cornbread Stuffing

Ingredients:

- 1 batch of cornbread (about 8 cups crumbled)*
- 4 tablespoons unsalted butter
- 1 large onion, diced
- 4 ribs celery, diced
- 2 cloves garlic, minced
- 1 teaspoon dried sage
- 1 teaspoon dried thyme
- 1/2 teaspoon dried rosemary
- 1/2 teaspoon dried marjoram
- Salt and black pepper to taste
- 2 cups chicken or vegetable broth
- 2 large eggs, beaten
- Chopped fresh parsley, for garnish (optional)

Instructions:

Prepare the Cornbread:
- Bake a batch of cornbread according to your favorite recipe or package instructions. Allow the cornbread to cool completely, then crumble it into a large mixing bowl. You should have about 8 cups of crumbled cornbread.

Saute the Aromatics:
- In a large skillet or frying pan, melt the unsalted butter over medium heat.
- Add the diced onion and celery to the skillet and cook until softened, about 5-7 minutes.
- Add the minced garlic to the skillet and cook for an additional 1-2 minutes until fragrant.

Mix the Stuffing:
- Transfer the sautéed aromatics to the bowl with the crumbled cornbread. Mix until well combined.

Moisten the Stuffing:
- Gradually pour the chicken or vegetable broth over the cornbread mixture, stirring well to combine. The mixture should be moistened but not overly soggy.
- Taste and adjust the seasoning with salt and black pepper if necessary.

Add Eggs:

- Stir in the beaten eggs until evenly distributed throughout the stuffing mixture. This will help bind the stuffing together during baking.

Bake the Stuffing:
- Preheat your oven to 350°F (175°C).
- Transfer the stuffing mixture to a greased 9x13-inch baking dish or a similar-sized casserole dish, spreading it out evenly.
- Cover the dish with aluminum foil and bake in the preheated oven for 30 minutes.

Finish Baking:
- Remove the foil and bake for an additional 15-20 minutes, or until the top of the stuffing is golden brown and crispy.

Garnish and Serve:
- Once baked, remove the cornbread stuffing from the oven.
- Garnish with chopped fresh parsley, if desired, before serving.

Enjoy:
- Serve the cornbread stuffing hot as a delicious and comforting side dish, perfect for Thanksgiving, Christmas, or any festive meal!

This recipe yields flavorful and moist cornbread stuffing with a golden-brown crust, making it a classic holiday favorite that pairs well with roasted turkey, chicken, or pork. Adjust the seasoning and add-ins according to your taste preferences.

Fried Chicken Wings

Ingredients:

- 2 lbs (about 900g) chicken wings, separated into flats and drumettes
- 1 cup buttermilk
- 1 cup all-purpose flour
- 1 teaspoon garlic powder
- 1 teaspoon onion powder
- 1 teaspoon paprika
- 1 teaspoon salt, plus more to taste
- 1/2 teaspoon black pepper
- Vegetable oil, for frying
- Optional: hot sauce, for serving

Instructions:

Marinate the Chicken Wings:
- Place the chicken wings in a large bowl and pour the buttermilk over them. Toss to coat the wings evenly. Cover the bowl with plastic wrap and let the wings marinate in the refrigerator for at least 1 hour, or overnight for best results.

Prepare the Coating:
- In a shallow dish, mix together the all-purpose flour, garlic powder, onion powder, paprika, salt, and black pepper until well combined.

Coat the Chicken Wings:
- Remove the marinated chicken wings from the buttermilk, allowing any excess buttermilk to drip off.
- Dredge each wing in the seasoned flour mixture, ensuring it is evenly coated. Shake off any excess flour.

Fry the Chicken Wings:
- In a large skillet or deep fryer, heat vegetable oil to 350°F (175°C).
- Carefully add the coated chicken wings to the hot oil in batches, making sure not to overcrowd the pan.
- Fry the wings for about 10-12 minutes, turning occasionally, until they are golden brown and crispy and the internal temperature reaches 165°F (75°C).

Drain and Season:
- Use a slotted spoon or tongs to transfer the fried chicken wings to a wire rack or paper towel-lined plate to drain any excess oil.
- Immediately sprinkle the hot wings with a little more salt to taste.

Serve:
- Serve the fried chicken wings hot as they are or toss them in your favorite hot sauce for extra flavor.

- Optionally, serve with celery sticks and blue cheese or ranch dressing for dipping.

Enjoy:
- Enjoy these crispy and flavorful fried chicken wings as a delicious appetizer, snack, or main dish!

This recipe yields crispy and succulent fried chicken wings with a perfectly seasoned coating, making them an irresistible favorite for parties, game days, or any casual gathering. Adjust the seasoning and frying time according to your taste preferences.

Sweet Potato Casserole

Ingredients:

For the Sweet Potato Filling:

- 4-5 medium sweet potatoes
- 1/2 cup unsalted butter, melted
- 1/2 cup brown sugar, packed
- 2 large eggs, beaten
- 1/4 cup milk
- 1 teaspoon vanilla extract
- 1/2 teaspoon ground cinnamon
- 1/4 teaspoon ground nutmeg
- 1/4 teaspoon salt

For the Topping:

- 1 cup brown sugar, packed
- 1/2 cup all-purpose flour
- 1/3 cup unsalted butter, melted
- 1 cup chopped pecans or walnuts

Instructions:

Prepare the Sweet Potatoes:
- Preheat your oven to 375°F (190°C).
- Wash the sweet potatoes and pierce them several times with a fork.
- Place the sweet potatoes on a baking sheet and bake in the preheated oven for about 45-60 minutes, or until they are tender. Allow them to cool slightly.

Make the Sweet Potato Filling:
- Once the sweet potatoes are cool enough to handle, peel off the skins and place the flesh in a large mixing bowl.
- Mash the sweet potatoes with a potato masher or fork until smooth.
- Add the melted butter, brown sugar, beaten eggs, milk, vanilla extract, ground cinnamon, ground nutmeg, and salt to the bowl. Mix until well combined.

Assemble the Casserole:
- Transfer the sweet potato filling to a greased 9x13-inch baking dish, spreading it out evenly.

Prepare the Topping:
- In a separate mixing bowl, combine the brown sugar, all-purpose flour, melted butter, and chopped pecans or walnuts. Mix until the topping is crumbly and well combined.

Add the Topping:
- Sprinkle the topping mixture evenly over the sweet potato filling in the baking dish.

Bake the Casserole:
- Bake the sweet potato casserole in the preheated oven for about 25-30 minutes, or until the topping is golden brown and the filling is set.

Serve:
- Once baked, remove the sweet potato casserole from the oven and let it cool for a few minutes before serving.

Enjoy:
- Serve the sweet potato casserole hot as a delicious and comforting side dish, perfect for holiday dinners or any special occasion!

This recipe yields a rich and flavorful sweet potato casserole with a creamy filling and crunchy topping, making it a favorite side dish for Thanksgiving, Christmas, or any festive meal. Adjust the sweetness and seasoning according to your taste preferences.

Chicken Fried Steak

Ingredients:

For the Steak:

- 4 beef cube steaks (about 4 ounces each), tenderized
- 1 cup all-purpose flour
- 1 teaspoon garlic powder
- 1 teaspoon onion powder
- 1 teaspoon paprika
- 1 teaspoon salt
- 1/2 teaspoon black pepper
- 2 large eggs
- 1/4 cup milk
- Vegetable oil, for frying

For the Gravy:

- 1/4 cup pan drippings (from frying the steak)
- 1/4 cup all-purpose flour
- 2 cups milk
- Salt and black pepper to taste

Instructions:

Prepare the Steak:
- In a shallow dish, combine the all-purpose flour, garlic powder, onion powder, paprika, salt, and black pepper. Mix well.
- In another shallow dish, beat the eggs with milk to create an egg wash.
- Dredge each cube steak in the seasoned flour, shaking off any excess.
- Dip the floured steak into the egg wash, then dredge it in the seasoned flour again, coating it evenly. Repeat with all the steaks.

Fry the Steak:
- In a large skillet or frying pan, heat about 1/4 inch of vegetable oil over medium-high heat until hot.
- Carefully add the breaded cube steaks to the hot oil, working in batches if necessary to avoid overcrowding the pan.
- Fry the steaks for about 3-4 minutes on each side, or until golden brown and crispy.

- Once cooked, transfer the fried steaks to a paper towel-lined plate to drain any excess oil. Keep them warm while you prepare the gravy.

Make the Gravy:
- Pour off all but about 1/4 cup of the pan drippings from the skillet.
- Add the 1/4 cup of flour to the skillet with the pan drippings, stirring to create a roux. Cook the roux over medium heat for about 1-2 minutes, until it turns golden brown.
- Gradually whisk in the milk, stirring constantly to prevent lumps from forming.
- Continue cooking the gravy, stirring constantly, until it thickens to your desired consistency. Season with salt and black pepper to taste.

Serve:
- Serve the chicken fried steak hot with the creamy gravy spooned over the top.

Enjoy:
- Enjoy this classic Southern dish with mashed potatoes, biscuits, or your favorite side dishes for a hearty and satisfying meal!

This recipe yields crispy and flavorful chicken fried steak with a creamy and rich gravy, perfect for a comforting dinner at home. Adjust the seasoning and thickness of the gravy according to your taste preferences.

Pecan Pie

Ingredients:

- 1 9-inch unbaked pie crust (homemade or store-bought)

For the Filling:

- 1 cup light corn syrup
- 3/4 cup packed brown sugar
- 3 large eggs
- 1/4 cup unsalted butter, melted
- 1 teaspoon vanilla extract
- 1 1/2 cups pecan halves

Instructions:

Preheat the Oven:
- Preheat your oven to 350°F (175°C).

Prepare the Pie Crust:
- Place the unbaked pie crust in a 9-inch pie dish. Crimp or flute the edges as desired.

Make the Filling:
- In a large mixing bowl, combine the light corn syrup, packed brown sugar, beaten eggs, melted butter, and vanilla extract. Mix until well combined.
- Stir in the pecan halves until they are evenly coated with the syrup mixture.

Fill the Pie Crust:
- Pour the pecan filling into the unbaked pie crust, spreading it out evenly.

Bake the Pie:
- Place the filled pie crust on a baking sheet to catch any drips.
- Bake the pecan pie in the preheated oven for about 50-60 minutes, or until the filling is set and the crust is golden brown. You can check for doneness by gently jiggling the pie - the center should be firm but still slightly jiggly.

Cool and Serve:
- Once baked, remove the pecan pie from the oven and let it cool completely on a wire rack before serving.
- Optionally, serve the pie with whipped cream or vanilla ice cream for an extra indulgent treat.

Enjoy:

- Slice and serve the pecan pie at room temperature as a deliciously sweet and nutty dessert, perfect for holidays, gatherings, or any special occasion!

This recipe yields a classic pecan pie with a gooey, sweet filling and crunchy pecan topping, all encased in a flaky pie crust. Adjust the sweetness by using dark corn syrup or adding more or less brown sugar according to your taste preferences.

Chicken and Dumplings

Ingredients:

For the Chicken and Broth:

- 1 whole chicken (about 3-4 pounds), cut into pieces
- 8 cups chicken broth
- 1 onion, chopped
- 2 carrots, chopped
- 2 celery stalks, chopped
- 3 cloves garlic, minced
- 2 bay leaves
- Salt and black pepper to taste

For the Dumplings:

- 2 cups all-purpose flour
- 1 tablespoon baking powder
- 1 teaspoon salt
- 1/4 cup unsalted butter, cold and cubed
- 3/4 cup milk

Instructions:

Prepare the Chicken and Broth:
- In a large pot or Dutch oven, combine the chicken pieces, chicken broth, chopped onion, chopped carrots, chopped celery, minced garlic, and bay leaves.
- Season with salt and black pepper to taste.
- Bring the mixture to a boil over medium-high heat, then reduce the heat to low and let it simmer for about 1 hour, or until the chicken is cooked through and tender.

Shred the Chicken:
- Once the chicken is cooked, remove it from the pot and let it cool slightly.
- Remove the skin and bones from the chicken pieces, then shred the meat using two forks or your fingers. Discard the skin and bones.

Make the Dumplings:
- In a mixing bowl, combine the all-purpose flour, baking powder, and salt.

- Cut in the cold, cubed butter using a pastry cutter or your fingers until the mixture resembles coarse crumbs.
- Gradually stir in the milk until a soft dough forms.

Roll and Cut the Dumplings:
- On a floured surface, roll out the dough to about 1/4-inch thickness.
- Use a knife or pizza cutter to cut the dough into squares or rectangles, about 1 to 2 inches in size.

Cook the Dumplings:
- Return the pot of broth to a gentle simmer over medium heat.
- Drop the dumplings into the simmering broth, a few at a time, stirring gently to prevent sticking.
- Cook the dumplings for about 10-15 minutes, or until they are cooked through and tender.

Add the Chicken:
- Once the dumplings are cooked, return the shredded chicken to the pot.
- Stir gently to combine and heat through.

Serve:
- Ladle the chicken and dumplings into bowls and serve hot.

Enjoy:
- Enjoy this comforting and hearty chicken and dumplings dish as a satisfying meal for any occasion!

This recipe yields a classic chicken and dumplings dish with tender shredded chicken, flavorful broth, and fluffy dumplings, making it a comforting and delicious meal that's perfect for cold days or anytime you crave a warm, home-cooked comfort food. Adjust the seasoning and thickness of the broth according to your taste preferences.

Grits with Cheese

Ingredients:

- 1 cup grits (stone-ground or quick-cooking)
- 4 cups water or chicken broth
- 1 cup shredded cheddar cheese
- 1/4 cup grated Parmesan cheese
- 1/4 cup unsalted butter
- Salt and black pepper to taste
- Optional: chopped green onions or chives for garnish

Instructions:

Cook the Grits:
- In a medium saucepan, bring the water or chicken broth to a boil over medium-high heat.
- Slowly whisk in the grits, stirring constantly to prevent lumps from forming.
- Reduce the heat to low and simmer, stirring occasionally, until the grits are thick and creamy. This will take about 20-30 minutes for stone-ground grits or 5-7 minutes for quick-cooking grits.

Add Cheese and Butter:
- Once the grits are cooked to your desired consistency, stir in the shredded cheddar cheese, grated Parmesan cheese, and unsalted butter.
- Continue stirring until the cheese and butter are fully melted and incorporated into the grits.

Season:
- Season the cheesy grits with salt and black pepper to taste. Adjust the seasoning as needed.

Serve:
- Transfer the cheesy grits to a serving bowl or individual plates.
- Garnish with chopped green onions or chives, if desired.

Enjoy:
- Serve the cheesy grits hot as a delicious and comforting side dish for breakfast, brunch, or any meal of the day!

This recipe yields creamy and flavorful cheesy grits with a rich and indulgent texture, perfect for serving alongside eggs, bacon, sausage, or your favorite breakfast items.

Customize the recipe by adding other types of cheese or additional seasonings according to your taste preferences.

Southern Style Coleslaw

Ingredients:

- 1 small head of green cabbage, shredded (about 4 cups)
- 1 large carrot, grated
- 1/2 cup mayonnaise
- 2 tablespoons apple cider vinegar
- 1 tablespoon Dijon mustard
- 1 tablespoon honey or granulated sugar
- 1/2 teaspoon celery seed
- Salt and black pepper to taste

Instructions:

Prepare the Vegetables:
- Shred the green cabbage using a sharp knife or a mandoline slicer. Alternatively, you can use a food processor fitted with a shredding attachment.
- Grate the carrot using a box grater or a food processor.

Make the Dressing:
- In a small bowl, whisk together the mayonnaise, apple cider vinegar, Dijon mustard, honey or sugar, and celery seed until well combined.

Combine the Coleslaw:
- In a large mixing bowl, combine the shredded cabbage and grated carrot.
- Pour the prepared dressing over the cabbage and carrot mixture.

Toss and Season:
- Toss the coleslaw ingredients together until the vegetables are evenly coated with the dressing.
- Season the coleslaw with salt and black pepper to taste. Adjust the seasoning as needed.

Chill:
- Cover the bowl with plastic wrap or transfer the coleslaw to an airtight container.
- Refrigerate the coleslaw for at least 1 hour before serving to allow the flavors to meld and the vegetables to soften slightly.

Serve:
- Give the coleslaw a final toss before serving.
- Serve the southern-style coleslaw as a refreshing side dish alongside barbecue, fried chicken, sandwiches, or any favorite Southern meal.

Enjoy:
- Enjoy the crisp and creamy texture of this classic southern-style coleslaw, bursting with flavor and perfect for any occasion!

This recipe yields a delicious and tangy southern-style coleslaw with a creamy dressing, crunchy cabbage, and sweet carrot, making it a versatile side dish that complements a wide range of main courses. Adjust the sweetness and tanginess of the dressing according to your taste preferences.

Sweet Tea

Ingredients:

- 4 family-sized tea bags (or 8 regular-sized tea bags)
- 8 cups water
- 1 cup granulated sugar (adjust to taste)
- Ice cubes
- Lemon slices or mint sprigs for garnish (optional)

Instructions:

Boil Water:
- In a large saucepan, bring 8 cups of water to a boil.

Steep Tea Bags:
- Once the water reaches a rolling boil, remove the saucepan from the heat.
- Add the tea bags to the hot water and let them steep for 5-7 minutes, depending on how strong you prefer your tea.

Sweeten the Tea:
- After steeping, remove the tea bags from the water and discard them.
- While the tea is still hot, stir in the granulated sugar until it is completely dissolved. Adjust the amount of sugar to your taste preference.

Chill:
- Allow the sweet tea to cool to room temperature.
- Once cooled, transfer the tea to a pitcher and refrigerate until cold. You can speed up the cooling process by placing the pitcher in the refrigerator or by adding ice cubes directly to the tea.

Serve:
- When ready to serve, fill glasses with ice cubes.
- Pour the chilled sweet tea over the ice in each glass.

Garnish (Optional):
- Garnish each glass with a slice of lemon or a sprig of fresh mint, if desired.

Enjoy:
- Serve the southern sweet tea as a refreshing and classic beverage, perfect for sipping on a hot day or with your favorite Southern meal!

This recipe yields a traditional southern sweet tea with just the right balance of sweetness and tea flavor. Adjust the sugar amount according to your preference for sweetness. You can also customize the tea by adding lemon slices or fresh mint for a hint of extra flavor.

Buttermilk Fried Shrimp

Ingredients:

- 1 pound large shrimp, peeled and deveined
- 1 cup buttermilk
- 1 cup all-purpose flour
- 1 teaspoon garlic powder
- 1 teaspoon paprika
- 1/2 teaspoon cayenne pepper (adjust to taste)
- Salt and black pepper to taste
- Vegetable oil, for frying
- Lemon wedges, for serving (optional)
- Cocktail sauce or tartar sauce, for dipping

Instructions:

Marinate the Shrimp:
- Place the peeled and deveined shrimp in a bowl and pour the buttermilk over them. Toss to coat the shrimp evenly.
- Cover the bowl with plastic wrap and let the shrimp marinate in the refrigerator for at least 30 minutes, or up to 2 hours for best results.

Prepare the Coating:
- In a shallow dish, combine the all-purpose flour, garlic powder, paprika, cayenne pepper, salt, and black pepper. Mix well to combine.

Coat the Shrimp:
- Remove the shrimp from the buttermilk marinade, allowing any excess buttermilk to drip off.
- Dredge each shrimp in the seasoned flour mixture, shaking off any excess.

Fry the Shrimp:
- In a large skillet or deep fryer, heat vegetable oil to 350°F (175°C).
- Carefully add the coated shrimp to the hot oil, working in batches if necessary to avoid overcrowding the pan.
- Fry the shrimp for about 2-3 minutes on each side, or until they are golden brown and crispy.
- Once cooked, use a slotted spoon or tongs to transfer the fried shrimp to a paper towel-lined plate to drain any excess oil.
- Repeat the frying process with the remaining shrimp.

Serve:
- Serve the buttermilk fried shrimp hot, garnished with lemon wedges if desired.
- Serve with cocktail sauce or tartar sauce on the side for dipping.

Enjoy:
- Enjoy the crispy and flavorful buttermilk fried shrimp as a delicious appetizer or main dish!

This recipe yields crispy and succulent buttermilk fried shrimp with a golden-brown crust, perfect for serving as an appetizer or main course. Adjust the seasoning and frying time according to your taste preferences and the size of the shrimp.

Country Fried Steak

Ingredients:

For the Steak:

- 4 beef cube steaks (about 4 ounces each)
- 1 cup all-purpose flour
- 2 teaspoons garlic powder
- 2 teaspoons onion powder
- 1 teaspoon paprika
- Salt and black pepper to taste
- 2 large eggs
- 1/4 cup milk
- Vegetable oil, for frying

For the Gravy:

- 1/4 cup pan drippings (from frying the steak)
- 1/4 cup all-purpose flour
- 2 cups milk
- Salt and black pepper to taste

Instructions:

Prepare the Steak:
- In a shallow dish, combine the all-purpose flour, garlic powder, onion powder, paprika, salt, and black pepper.
- In another shallow dish, beat the eggs with milk to create an egg wash.
- Season the cube steaks with salt and black pepper on both sides.

Dredge the Steak:
- Dredge each cube steak in the seasoned flour, shaking off any excess.
- Dip the floured steak into the egg wash, then dredge it in the seasoned flour again, coating it evenly. Repeat with all the steaks.

Fry the Steak:
- In a large skillet or frying pan, heat about 1/4 inch of vegetable oil over medium-high heat until hot.
- Carefully add the breaded cube steaks to the hot oil, working in batches if necessary to avoid overcrowding the pan.

- Fry the steaks for about 3-4 minutes on each side, or until golden brown and crispy.
- Once cooked, transfer the fried steaks to a paper towel-lined plate to drain any excess oil. Keep them warm while you prepare the gravy.

Make the Gravy:
- Pour off all but about 1/4 cup of the pan drippings from the skillet.
- Add the 1/4 cup of flour to the skillet with the pan drippings, stirring to create a roux. Cook the roux over medium heat for about 1-2 minutes, until it turns golden brown.
- Gradually whisk in the milk, stirring constantly to prevent lumps from forming.
- Continue cooking the gravy, stirring constantly, until it thickens to your desired consistency. Season with salt and black pepper to taste.

Serve:
- Serve the country fried steak hot, topped with the creamy gravy.

Enjoy:
- Enjoy this classic country fried steak dish with creamy gravy, served alongside mashed potatoes, biscuits, or your favorite sides!

This recipe yields crispy and flavorful country fried steak with a creamy and rich gravy, perfect for a comforting dinner at home. Adjust the seasoning and thickness of the gravy according to your taste preferences.

Dirty Rice

Ingredients:

- 1 cup long-grain white rice
- 1 lb (about 450g) ground pork or chicken
- 1 medium onion, finely chopped
- 1 bell pepper, finely chopped
- 2 celery stalks, finely chopped
- 3 cloves garlic, minced
- 1 cup chicken broth
- 2 tablespoons vegetable oil
- 2 teaspoons Cajun seasoning (adjust to taste)
- 1 teaspoon paprika
- 1/2 teaspoon dried thyme
- 1/2 teaspoon dried oregano
- Salt and black pepper to taste
- Chopped green onions or parsley for garnish (optional)

Instructions:

Cook the Rice:
- Rinse the rice under cold water until the water runs clear.
- In a medium saucepan, combine the rice with 2 cups of water and a pinch of salt.
- Bring to a boil, then reduce the heat to low, cover, and simmer for about 18-20 minutes, or until the rice is cooked and tender. Remove from heat and let it sit covered for 5 minutes. Fluff with a fork and set aside.

Prepare the Meat Mixture:
- In a large skillet or frying pan, heat the vegetable oil over medium heat.
- Add the ground pork or chicken to the skillet and cook, breaking it apart with a spatula, until browned and cooked through.
- Add the chopped onion, bell pepper, and celery to the skillet. Cook, stirring occasionally, until the vegetables are softened, about 5-7 minutes.
- Add the minced garlic to the skillet and cook for an additional 1-2 minutes until fragrant.

Season the Mixture:
- Stir in the Cajun seasoning, paprika, dried thyme, and dried oregano until well combined.
- Season with salt and black pepper to taste.

Combine Rice and Meat Mixture:
- Add the cooked rice to the skillet with the meat and vegetable mixture.
- Pour in the chicken broth and stir everything together until evenly combined.

Simmer and Serve:
- Reduce the heat to low and let the mixture simmer, stirring occasionally, for about 10-15 minutes, or until the flavors are well blended and the rice has absorbed some of the liquid.
- If the mixture seems too dry, you can add a little more chicken broth as needed.

Garnish and Serve:
- Once ready, remove the skillet from the heat.
- Garnish the dirty rice with chopped green onions or parsley, if desired.
- Serve hot as a delicious and flavorful side dish or main course.

Enjoy:
- Enjoy this classic Louisiana dish packed with savory flavors and hearty ingredients, perfect for a comforting meal any time of the year!

This recipe yields a flavorful and satisfying dirty rice dish with a perfect balance of meat, vegetables, and spices. Adjust the seasoning and spice level according to your taste preferences.

Fried Oysters

Ingredients:

- 1 dozen fresh oysters, shucked
- 1 cup all-purpose flour
- 2 eggs, beaten
- 1 cup fine breadcrumbs or cornmeal
- Salt and black pepper to taste
- Vegetable oil, for frying
- Lemon wedges, for serving
- Cocktail sauce or tartar sauce, for dipping

Instructions:

Prepare the Oysters:
- Rinse the shucked oysters under cold water and pat them dry with paper towels.
- Season the oysters lightly with salt and black pepper.

Set Up Breading Station:
- Set up a breading station with three shallow dishes: one with all-purpose flour, one with beaten eggs, and one with breadcrumbs or cornmeal.

Bread the Oysters:
- Dredge each oyster in the flour, shaking off any excess.
- Dip the floured oyster into the beaten eggs, ensuring it is coated evenly.
- Finally, coat the oyster in breadcrumbs or cornmeal, pressing gently to adhere. Repeat with all the oysters.

Heat Oil for Frying:
- In a large skillet or frying pan, heat vegetable oil to 350°F (175°C) over medium-high heat.

Fry the Oysters:
- Carefully add the breaded oysters to the hot oil, working in batches if necessary to avoid overcrowding the pan.
- Fry the oysters for about 2-3 minutes on each side, or until they are golden brown and crispy.
- Once cooked, use a slotted spoon or tongs to transfer the fried oysters to a paper towel-lined plate to drain any excess oil. Keep them warm while you fry the remaining batches.

Serve:
- Serve the fried oysters hot, garnished with lemon wedges.
- Serve with cocktail sauce or tartar sauce on the side for dipping.

Enjoy:

- Enjoy the crispy and succulent fried oysters as a delicious appetizer or main dish!

This recipe yields crispy and flavorful fried oysters with a golden-brown crust and tender interior, perfect for serving as an appetizer or main course. Adjust the seasoning and frying time according to your taste preferences.

Texas Toast

Ingredients:

- Thick-sliced white bread (such as Texas toast bread or French bread)
- 1/2 cup unsalted butter, softened
- 2 cloves garlic, minced (optional)
- 1 tablespoon finely chopped parsley (optional)
- Salt to taste

Instructions:

Prepare the Garlic Butter:
- In a small bowl, combine the softened butter, minced garlic (if using), chopped parsley (if using), and a pinch of salt. Mix until well combined.

Spread Garlic Butter on Bread:
- Preheat your oven to 375°F (190°C).
- Place the thick-sliced white bread on a baking sheet lined with parchment paper or aluminum foil.
- Spread a generous amount of the garlic butter mixture on one side of each slice of bread.

Bake the Texas Toast:
- Place the baking sheet in the preheated oven and bake the Texas toast for about 8-10 minutes, or until the bread is golden brown and crispy on the edges.

Serve:
- Once baked, remove the Texas toast from the oven and let it cool slightly.
- Serve the warm Texas toast as a delicious side dish or accompaniment to soups, salads, pasta, or any main course.

Enjoy:
- Enjoy the buttery and garlicky flavor of homemade Texas toast as a tasty addition to your meals!

This recipe yields golden-brown and flavorful Texas toast with a crispy exterior and a soft, buttery interior. Adjust the amount of garlic, parsley, and salt in the butter mixture according to your taste preferences. Serve the Texas toast warm for the best texture and flavor.

Collard Green and Black-eyed Pea Soup

Ingredients:

- 1 tablespoon olive oil
- 1 onion, chopped
- 3 cloves garlic, minced
- 2 carrots, diced
- 2 celery stalks, diced
- 1 bell pepper, diced
- 8 cups vegetable or chicken broth
- 2 cups cooked black-eyed peas (canned or cooked from dried)
- 1 bunch collard greens, stems removed and leaves chopped
- 1 teaspoon smoked paprika
- 1/2 teaspoon cayenne pepper (adjust to taste)
- Salt and black pepper to taste
- Lemon wedges, for serving (optional)

Instructions:

Sauté Aromatics:
- In a large pot or Dutch oven, heat the olive oil over medium heat.
- Add the chopped onion, minced garlic, diced carrots, diced celery, and diced bell pepper to the pot. Sauté for 5-7 minutes, or until the vegetables are softened and fragrant.

Add Broth and Black-eyed Peas:
- Pour in the vegetable or chicken broth, along with the cooked black-eyed peas.
- Bring the mixture to a simmer over medium heat.

Cook Collard Greens:
- Add the chopped collard greens to the pot.
- Simmer the soup for about 15-20 minutes, or until the collard greens are tender.

Season the Soup:
- Stir in the smoked paprika and cayenne pepper.
- Season the soup with salt and black pepper to taste. Adjust the seasoning as needed.

Serve:
- Ladle the collard greens and black-eyed pea soup into bowls.

- Serve hot, with lemon wedges on the side for squeezing over the soup, if desired.

Enjoy:
- Enjoy this hearty and nutritious collard greens and black-eyed pea soup as a comforting meal on a cold day!

This recipe yields a flavorful and wholesome soup with tender collard greens, creamy black-eyed peas, and aromatic vegetables, perfect for serving as a main course or starter. Customize the soup by adding additional spices or vegetables according to your taste preferences.

BBQ Pulled Pork

Ingredients:

- 3-4 lbs (1.4-1.8 kg) pork shoulder or pork butt
- 2 tablespoons brown sugar
- 2 teaspoons smoked paprika
- 1 teaspoon garlic powder
- 1 teaspoon onion powder
- 1 teaspoon ground cumin
- 1 teaspoon chili powder
- 1/2 teaspoon cayenne pepper (optional, for heat)
- Salt and black pepper to taste
- 1 cup barbecue sauce (homemade or store-bought)
- 1 cup chicken broth or water
- Hamburger buns or sandwich rolls, for serving
- Coleslaw, for topping (optional)

Instructions:

Prepare the Pork:
- In a small bowl, mix together the brown sugar, smoked paprika, garlic powder, onion powder, ground cumin, chili powder, cayenne pepper (if using), salt, and black pepper to create a dry rub.
- Rub the dry rub all over the pork shoulder or pork butt, covering it evenly.

Slow Cook the Pork:
- Place the seasoned pork in a slow cooker.
- Pour the chicken broth or water around the pork.
- Cover and cook on low heat for 8-10 hours, or on high heat for 4-6 hours, until the pork is very tender and easily shreds with a fork.

Shred the Pork:
- Once the pork is cooked, remove it from the slow cooker and transfer it to a cutting board.
- Use two forks to shred the pork into bite-sized pieces, discarding any excess fat.

Add BBQ Sauce:
- In a saucepan, heat the barbecue sauce over medium heat.
- Add the shredded pork to the saucepan and stir to coat the pork evenly with the barbecue sauce.
- Cook for an additional 5-10 minutes, stirring occasionally, until the pork is heated through and infused with the barbecue flavor.

Serve:

- Serve the BBQ pulled pork hot on hamburger buns or sandwich rolls.
- Optionally, top the pulled pork with coleslaw for extra flavor and texture.

Enjoy:

- Enjoy the delicious and tender BBQ pulled pork sandwiches as a satisfying meal for any occasion!

This recipe yields succulent and flavorful BBQ pulled pork with a perfect balance of smoky, sweet, and tangy flavors. Serve the pulled pork sandwiches with your favorite side dishes, such as coleslaw, potato salad, or baked beans, for a complete meal. Adjust the seasoning and barbecue sauce according to your taste preferences.

Cajun Shrimp Pasta

Ingredients:

- 8 oz (225g) linguine or fettuccine pasta
- 1 lb (450g) large shrimp, peeled and deveined
- 2 tablespoons Cajun seasoning
- 2 tablespoons olive oil
- 4 cloves garlic, minced
- 1 onion, finely chopped
- 1 bell pepper, thinly sliced
- 1 cup cherry tomatoes, halved
- 1 cup heavy cream
- 1/2 cup grated Parmesan cheese
- Salt and black pepper to taste
- Fresh parsley, chopped, for garnish

Instructions:

Cook the Pasta:
- Cook the pasta according to the package instructions until al dente. Drain and set aside.

Season and Cook the Shrimp:
- In a medium bowl, toss the peeled and deveined shrimp with Cajun seasoning until evenly coated.
- Heat olive oil in a large skillet over medium-high heat.
- Add the seasoned shrimp to the skillet and cook for 2-3 minutes per side, or until they are pink and cooked through. Remove the shrimp from the skillet and set aside.

Sauté Aromatics and Vegetables:
- In the same skillet, add minced garlic, finely chopped onion, and thinly sliced bell pepper. Sauté for 3-4 minutes, or until the vegetables are softened.

Add Tomatoes and Cream:
- Add halved cherry tomatoes to the skillet and cook for another 2 minutes.
- Pour in the heavy cream and bring to a simmer. Let it simmer for 2-3 minutes to thicken slightly.

Combine Pasta and Sauce:
- Return the cooked pasta to the skillet with the sauce. Toss until the pasta is well coated with the creamy sauce.

Add Shrimp and Cheese:
- Add the cooked shrimp back to the skillet.
- Sprinkle grated Parmesan cheese over the pasta and shrimp. Stir until the cheese is melted and the shrimp is heated through.

Season and Garnish:
- Season the Cajun shrimp pasta with salt and black pepper to taste.
- Garnish with chopped fresh parsley for added freshness and color.

Serve:
- Serve the Cajun shrimp pasta hot, garnished with additional Parmesan cheese and parsley if desired.

Enjoy:
- Enjoy this flavorful and comforting Cajun shrimp pasta as a delicious main course!

This recipe yields a creamy and spicy Cajun shrimp pasta with perfectly cooked shrimp, tender vegetables, and a flavorful sauce that coats every strand of pasta. Adjust the Cajun seasoning according to your taste preferences for more or less heat. Serve the pasta with garlic bread or a side salad for a complete meal.

Baked Beans

Ingredients:

- 2 cups dried navy beans or pinto beans
- 6 cups water
- 1 onion, finely chopped
- 1/2 cup molasses
- 1/4 cup brown sugar
- 1/4 cup ketchup
- 2 tablespoons mustard
- 2 tablespoons Worcestershire sauce
- 1 teaspoon salt
- 1/2 teaspoon black pepper
- 4 slices bacon, chopped (optional)
- 1/2 cup barbecue sauce (optional)

Instructions:

Prepare the Beans:
- Rinse the dried beans under cold water and remove any debris or stones.
- In a large pot, cover the beans with water and soak overnight. Alternatively, you can use the quick soak method by bringing the beans to a boil, then removing them from heat and letting them soak for 1 hour.

Cook the Beans:
- After soaking, drain and rinse the beans.
- In a large pot or Dutch oven, combine the soaked beans with 6 cups of fresh water.
- Bring the beans to a boil, then reduce the heat to low and simmer for about 1 to 1 1/2 hours, or until the beans are tender but not mushy. Drain and set aside.

Prepare the Sauce:
- Preheat your oven to 325°F (160°C).
- In a mixing bowl, combine the finely chopped onion, molasses, brown sugar, ketchup, mustard, Worcestershire sauce, salt, and black pepper. Mix until well combined.

Combine Beans and Sauce:
- In a large baking dish or casserole dish, layer the cooked beans and chopped bacon (if using).
- Pour the prepared sauce mixture over the beans and bacon, ensuring that the beans are evenly coated with the sauce.

Bake the Beans:

- Cover the baking dish with aluminum foil and bake in the preheated oven for about 2 to 2 1/2 hours, or until the beans are tender and the sauce is thickened.
- If desired, uncover the beans during the last 30 minutes of baking to allow the top to brown slightly.

Optional BBQ Variation:
- If you prefer a barbecue flavor, you can stir in 1/2 cup of your favorite barbecue sauce along with the other sauce ingredients before baking.

Serve:
- Serve the baked beans hot as a delicious side dish for barbecues, picnics, or any meal of your choice.

Enjoy:
- Enjoy the rich and flavorful homemade baked beans, packed with hearty beans and a sweet and tangy sauce!

This recipe yields classic homemade baked beans with a sweet and savory sauce that's perfect for serving as a side dish at any gathering or barbecue. Adjust the sweetness and seasoning according to your taste preferences.

www.ingramcontent.com/pod-product-compliance
Lightning Source LLC
LaVergne TN
LVHW081605060526
838201LV00054B/2081